D0119717

Withdrawn

BRITAIN'S NATIONAL PARKS

Edited and with an Introduction by
MERVYN BELL

Contributors:
Sylvia Sayer   S. H. Burton
Margaret Davies   John Barrett
William Condry   Patrick Monkhouse
C. H. D. Acland   Arthur Raistrick
Harry Mead   J. S. Allen
John Foster

DAVID & CHARLES

NEWTON ABBOT   LONDON   NORTH POMFRET (VT)

ISBN 0 7153 6792 7 (hardback)
0 7153 7920 8 (paperback)
Library of Congress Catalog Card Number 74–20450

First published 1975
Second impression 1979
First published in paperback 1979

© Mervyn Bell, Sylvia Sayer, S. H. Burton, Margaret Davies,
John Barrett, William Condry, Patrick Monkhouse,
C. H. D. Acland, Arthur Raistrick, Harry Mead, J. S. Allen,
and John Foster for their respective contributions, 1975

Printed in Great Britain
by Redwood Burn Ltd, Trowbridge & Esher
for David & Charles (Publishers) Limited
Brunel House Newton Abbot Devon

Published in the United States of America
by David & Charles Inc
North Pomfret Vermont 05053 USA

CONTENTS

INTRODUCTION

Mervyn Bell

Recognising the inevitability of further change to the native beauty of the Lakeland landscape, Wordsworth ended his *Guide through the District of the Lakes* by explaining how to safeguard its inherent qualities and claiming that the district should be deemed 'a sort of national property, in which every man has an interest who has an eye to perceive and a heart to enjoy'. But more than a century was to pass before Parliament concerned itself with the protection of Britain's natural heritage, before the Lake District and other areas of outstanding scenery were specially protected for the nation as national parks.

It was in the late eighteenth century that people began travelling to the wilder parts of the country for holidays, as improvements to turnpike roads and bridges made long journeys by horsedrawn coach possible. They went to view the mountains from the valleys and to discover for themselves the qualities of the landscape so vividly portrayed for them by artists, writers and poets. Mountains were no longer 'awful' but part of man's natural home and a new appreciation of the responsibilities that attend his relationship with nature was beginning to be accepted. During the years that passed between Wordsworth's claim and eventual legislation, reformers and voluntary societies developed the ideas which have led to the modern concepts of landscape conservation for aesthetic and recreational reasons and nature conservation for scientific ones.

The coming of the railway age enabled the ordinary citizen to follow the well-to-do to the hills and to the seaside for peace and for pleasure, and for welcome relief from the dirt, the noise and tension of crowded factories, mills and back-to-back houses. In 1851, half the population of England already lived in towns; wakes weeks of factory closure in the North and Midlands and, from 1871, Bank Holidays gave millions some days of leisure. But they were by no means always welcomed in the countryside. Ramblers, outdoor naturalists and skilled climbers were readily accepted in the Lake District and Snowdonia. Elsewhere, as visitors from the towns, they were often unpopular for fear they would cause damage through ignorance of country ways, or they were turned away to protect the purity of water supplies or valuable sporting rights, and especially so from the grouse moors of northern England.

Despite the careless way in which the mines, waste tips, factories and mills of the Industrial Revolution had been set down without consideration for their surroundings, and despite fifty years of agricultural depression, much of the character of early eighteenth-century lowland Britain was preserved until after World War I. It retained its hardwood trees in woods and coverts, its hedges and parkland in the hands of family estates.

Townsmen formed groups to further their interests in the country and the earliest national societies, established in the 1830s, were mainly concerned with the study of plants and animals. The oldest of our amenity pressure groups, the

An engraving by George Hunt from a coloured aquatint after
J. E. Jones. It was in the late eighteenth century that improvements
to turnpike roads and bridges made longer journeys possible – the
tourist trade had begun

Commons, Open Spaces and Footpaths Preservation Society, was founded in 1865 and concentrated on maintaining and extending public rights of access to open country. James Bryce's Access to Mountains (Scotland) Bill of 1884 was the first of many unsuccessful attempts to legislate to give the public rights of access to uncultivated mountains and moors, but it was not until 1949 that a workable law was produced—and then only for England and Wales; Scotland had to wait until 1967.

Other groups were gradually formed to take direct action for the conservation of wildlife, historic buildings and landscape by acquiring and managing land. Prominent among them were the Royal Society for the Protection of Birds formed in 1891; the National Trust, 1895, for places of historic interest or natural beauty in England and Wales; the National Trust for Scotland, 1931; the Society for the Promotion of Nature Reserves, 1912; the County Naturalists' Trusts in England and Wales, of which Norfolk was the first in 1926; and the Scottish Wildlife Trust formed in 1965.

In spite of overlapping membership the groups tended to follow their own interests and not to promote a common cause, which would have strengthened their effectiveness politically. By the 1920s a demand for some form of country planning was emerging and it was the need to organise concerted action for the preservation of rural scenery and amenities that led to the formation of the Council for the Preservation of Rural England in 1926, the Association for the Preservation of Rural Scotland in 1927, and the Council for the Preservation of Rural Wales in 1928. The first mention of national parks in Parliament was a question in 1929 by Mr Macpherson calling attention 'to the project of securing for the nation in perpetuity some area in the Cairngorm range or elsewhere in Scotland for the free and unfettered use of the public and as a sanctuary for birds and animals...' But the Government's reply did nothing to further the creation of any national park.

The Council for the Preservation of Rural England followed quickly with a memorandum to the Prime Minister, Ramsay MacDonald, who then appointed a committee to examine the feasibility of establishing one or more national parks in Britain. Its report in 1931 reflected the financial crisis of the depression years; it agreed that there were large areas of exceptional natural interest which should be safeguarded for its own and future generations, but ruled out public acquisition and tentatively proposed schemes which depended on either £100,000 a year or £10,000 a year being found for five years from both public and private sources. The report was shelved.

'Country', however, appeared for the first time in the title of a planning statute with the Town and Country Planning Act, 1932. Local authorities were enabled, but not obliged, to plan land use in the countryside, to control the siting and design of factories and houses in it, to protect trees and woodlands from felling, and to secure the preservation of historic buildings. For the next ten years ministers replying to questions and debates about national parks were content to say that local authorities had powers to do much of what was needed. But the powers were not only optional ones, they were negative and difficult to operate; the authorities could only stop undesirable things happening.

The public campaign grew, with public meetings and demonstrations as well as lobbying. In 1932, a mass trespass organised by ramblers from both sides of the Pennines, and the sentencing of five of them to prison, highlighted the case for freedom to roam on the 215 square miles of uncultivated grouse moors in the Peak District. Members of all the outdoor societies south of the Border joined forces in 1935 to form the Standing Committee on National Parks. In 1943 the Scottish Council for National Parks was formed. Government remained apathetic, in spite of much better informed and represented public opinion, until the war concentrated thinking mightily.

During World War II the need to rebuild cities and to restore a prosperous countryside emphasised the interdependence of town and country and the need for central planning. A series of governmental committees prepared the way for post-war reconstruction. One of these, the Scott Committee on Land Utilisation in Rural Areas, reporting in 1942, brought together the planning of the countryside, public access to open country and rights of way, and the setting up of nature reserves and national parks which, it said, were long overdue in Britain.

After the war immense changes were made in the law of the land. First, the Town and Country Planning Act, 1947, applied a far-reaching new system of planning control throughout England and Wales and greatly strengthened its administration. It prohibited, with exceptions, the development or material change of use of land without the consent of one of the new county planning authorities. Similar changes were made in Scotland. Then the National Parks and Access to the Countryside Act was passed in 1949.

Main responsibility for the conservation of nature throughout Britain was accepted by central government and vested in the Nature Conservancy, which had been established earlier in the year by Royal Charter. The 1949 Act and its Royal Charter enabled the Nature Conservancy to establish and manage national nature reserves, to co-ordinate the setting up of forest and local nature reserves, and to define areas of special scientific interest to ensure consultation by planning authorities on development proposals that might affect them. And it has undertaken the scientific study and research which provide the basis for the management of wildlife and the environment.

The rest of the 1949 Act, however, did not apply to Scotland. It provided, in England and Wales, for national parks and the conservation of other landscapes of outstanding beauty, the securing of public access to open country, and dealing with rights of way on public paths. The National Parks Commission was established to designate national parks and keep the running of them under review, to designate areas of outstanding natural beauty, to propose long-distance routes for walkers and horse riders, and to provide information services and publicise a code of conduct for visitors to the countryside. Otherwise the Commission's role was advisory or supervisory; local government had the executive responsibilities.

In 1968 the Countryside Commission replaced the National Parks Commission and assumed its functions, with a wide brief to keep under review all matters relating to the provision and improvement of facilities for the enjoyment of the countryside in England and Wales; the conservation of its natural beauty and amenity; the need to secure public access for open-air recreation; and, for the first time, powers to carry out research and experiment.

Scotland had waited until 1967 for the law to be brought broadly into line with that south of the Border, except that there was no provision for national parks or areas of outstanding natural beauty. The Countryside Commission for Scotland was established too, with terms of reference very like those given next year to its southern counterpart.

There was considerable disappointment that the 1949 Act gave the National Parks Commission no powers to own and manage land in national parks—indeed no share in the running of the parks—and that the bill for them would not be paid by the Exchequer; both had been regarded as fundamental by two official reports. The basis for the legislation was a report by John Dower, made in 1945, which crystallised the thinking of the voluntary movement. He said:

A National Park may be defined, in application to Great Britain, as an extensive area of beautiful and relatively wild country in which, for the nation's benefit and by appropriate national decision and action, *a* the characteristic landscape beauty is strictly preserved, *b* access and facilities for public open-air enjoyment are amply provided, *c* wildlife and buildings and places of architectural and historic interest are suitably protected, while *d* established farming use is effectively maintained.

It was, Dower explained, only in the wilder country that the public at large desired, and could satisfactorily be given, a wide measure of recreational access. He estimated that the wilder country of England and Wales amounted to about one-fifth of the land area, 12,000 out of 58,000 square miles. But not all of this land was both beautiful and of sufficient extent which reduced the potential national park land to 8,000 square miles. This was the area that should be given special protection and he proposed ten national parks totalling 3,600 square miles. Twelve reserve areas totalled 4,400 square miles. Dower also listed a third category of amenity areas, not potential national parks, some of which deserved designated status as county or regional parks, or as forest or nature reserves.

The Hobhouse Committee, reporting in 1947, endorsed Dower's definition and developed his proposals in greater detail. It recommended twelve national parks covering 5,682 square miles, at least one of them to be within easy reach of the main centres of population. This intention is reflected in the statutory definition of national parks, which embodies the Committee's main criteria for their selection: 'great natural beauty, a high value for open-air recreation and substantial continuous extent'. Statu-

tory designation by the Commission, after confirmation by the Minister, establishes that it is (as nearly as possible in the words of the Act), 'especially desirable that the necessary measures shall be taken' for the purposes of 'preserving and enhancing the natural beauty' of the national parks and 'promoting their enjoyment by the public'.

The Commission was also responsible for designating areas of outstanding natural beauty. These derived from the Hobhouse Committee's proposals for 52 'conservation areas', areas of high scenic quality often combined with considerable scientific interest or value for recreation. The preservation of the natural beauty of an area included the preservation of its flora, fauna, and geological and physiographical fea-

In 1851 half the population of England already lived in towns;
a picnic and ramble in the countryside provided a welcome relief
from smut and smog

National Park	Date designation was confirmed	Area in square miles Dec 1974
Peak District	17. 4.51	542
Lake District	9. 5.51	866
Snowdonia	18.10.51	840
Dartmoor	30.10.51	365
Pembrokeshire Coast	29. 2.52	225
North York Moors	28.11.52	553
Yorkshire Dales	12.10.54	680
Exmoor	19.10.54	265
Northumberland	6. 4.56	398
Brecon Beacons	17. 4.57	519
		5,253*

* 9 per cent of the total area of England and Wales (58,350 square miles). 3,669 square miles in England; 7.3 per cent of England (50,333 square miles). 1,584 square miles in Wales; 19.7 per cent of Wales (8,017 square miles).

tures. But the 1949 Act was not designed to promote public recreation in areas of outstanding natural beauty, except by providing grants for the cost of securing access to open country, it concentrated on preserving and enhancing their natural beauty.

Between 1950 and 1955 the National Parks Commission made designation orders for ten of the twelve national parks recommended by the Hobhouse Committee, the last being confirmed in 1957. In the case of the Northumberland National Park, one of the Hobhouse conservation areas, the Cheviot Hills, was added with the intervening country to the best preserved part of the Roman Wall. The two national parks recommended by the Hobhouse Report but not designated were the South Downs and the Broads. The Commission found that widespread cultivation had too greatly reduced the recreational value of the South Downs and designated it an area of outstanding natural beauty. The Government was not prepared to face the cost of reclaiming the Broads and the

Commission ultimately decided that the scenery away from the water did not measure up to national park standards.

The Commission has formally considered designating two other areas as national parks, which were not in the Hobhouse list of twelve but were included among the fifty-two conservation areas. In 1972 a designation order was submitted to the Secretary of State for Wales for the Cambrian Mountains National Park; nearly a year later he rejected it because of the objections he had received. The Commission and supporters of the proposal were not given any opportunity to present their case at a public inquiry, much to the surprise and dismay of all who had wanted a national park in mid-Wales since Sir George Stapledon first suggested one in 1935.

The Cornish Coast was not designated a national park after careful study in the 1950s. The long narrow strips of coast were not sufficiently continuous and difficulties of administration were deemed too great. They were, however, designated an area of outstanding natural beauty.

The ten existing national parks are distinguished from other designated areas by being extensive areas of great scenic beauty in the wilder parts of England and Wales, which contain large stretches of uncultivated hill-farming land where open-air recreation can be combined with other uses. Designation establishes their national significance. It does not alter the ownership of any land; private, public and Crown land is included. It does not confer any new rights of access. Designation brings into force special arrangements for giving effect to the twin statutory purposes of preserving the natural beauty of the national parks and promoting their enjoyment.

Special arrangements are made for local planning authorities to run the parks and be responsible for development planning, development control and its enforcement under the Town and Country Planning Acts; providing and managing access and facilities for public enjoyment, principally under the 1949 Act and the Countryside Act, 1968; public relations work, including information and educative services; and, usually, public footpaths and bridleways, and traffic management.

Over the years the form which these administrative arrangements have taken in the different parks has considerably influenced the progress made towards achieving the twin purposes of the Statute. The Hobhouse Committee had wanted an autonomous park committee, with its own planning officer and staff, to be the local organisation for planning and managing each park. Half the members were to be appointed by the local authorities, the other half and the chairman by the National Parks Commission. The Commission was to own and manage land in the parks and to pay the cost of the committees. But the 1949 Act left executive responsibility for running the parks to the new local planning authorities and to the minister. One-third of the members was chosen by the minister, the other two-thirds by the local authorities.

Four of the parks were wholly within the area of a single county: Dartmoor, the Pembrokeshire Coast, the North York Moors and Northumberland. Six were in parts of two or more counties: Exmoor, the Brecon Beacons, Snowdonia, the Peak, the Lakes and the Yorkshire Dales. The Act was designed to ensure that a special planning committee of the county council was appointed for each single-county park and a joint planning board constituted for each multi-county park. Every park was to be run as a unit, free from other county business and not split into separate county pieces.

Application of the scheme to the single-county parks caused no difficulty. But nearly all the county councils objected to the transfer of their responsibilities for part of their territory to a joint board, although county council membership of it would be in a majority of two to one. Ministers began by resisting the county council objections, so the first two multi-county parks designated, the Peak and the Lake District, had joint boards. They did not insist that an independent national park planning officer be appointed for each (as had been promised in Parliament by the Government spokesman when resisting an amendment to make it mandatory). The Peak Board decided to appoint its own director-planning officer. The Lakes Board preferred to rely on the services of the planning staff of the constituent county councils. Ministers gave way to the objections of the county councils concerned with the other four multi-county parks, so Snowdonia (whose joint advisory committee appointed its own planning consultant), the Yorkshire Dales, Exmoor and the Brecon Beacons had the multi-committee administration which was criticised for the next twenty years as cumbersome and time wasting for members and staff.

Since local government was to run the parks, local government had to pay the bills. To encourage the park authorities to carry out the purposes for which the parks had been designated, the 1949 Act provided Exchequer grants of up to 75 per cent of the cost for specific actions, such as planting trees and removing eyesores to preserve and enhance natural beauty, securing access in open country, providing warden services, car parks, camping sites and accommodation, and (by contribution from the Commission) information services. But administration, inevitably the main single continuing item of cost, attracted no grant and threw an unfair burden on the local rates. The Commission repeatedly pointed out what a brake on progress this was proving. Moreover, in eight of the national parks the initiative, the decision whether to act or not to act if it involved expenditure, was taken not by the park committees but by their county councils and weighed against all the other claims on the county budget—for education, public health, police, roads and many other services. Only the two boards could take their own decisions, although even they were limited to amounts they considered reasonable to demand from their constituent counties.

Hopes were raised in 1969 when the Redcliffe-Maud Commission on Local Government in England and Wales recommended that every national park should be administered by a special authority, employing its own staff and recovering its expenses from the authorities in whose area it lay. The Commission had concluded that the purposes of the national parks were of a special kind in view of their national character. One Government accepted these proposals in a White Paper of 1970, but the next in a further White Paper in 1971 stated that, 'In the Government's view, very little change is needed in the present statutory provisions governing planning functions in national parks.'

The Countryside Commission replied with a report by Sir Jack Longland which explained in detail the reasons for its whole-hearted support for the Redcliffe-Maud proposals. It asked again that the Exchequer should bear a much greater share of the costs. However, a few months later, judging that its preferred solution would not be implemented by the Government which had decided to give much greater responsibilities to local authorities, the Commission negotiated an agreement with the County Councils Association. This became the basis for provisions included in the Local Government Act, 1972, which greatly improved park administration. Since 1 April 1974 every national park has been administered by a single executive committee or board, which appoints its own national park officer. At the same time the financial support for the parks was much increased.

Specific Exchequer grants were replaced by rate support grant, and a special national park supplementary block grant began by which the Exchequer contributes 75 per cent of the estimated net expenditure of each park authority including the cost of staff. The Commission continues to contribute up to 80 per cent of the cost of park information and educative services. It may also contribute to the cost of other park work which it particularly wants to encourage.

Two national parks have boards: the Peak District, a multi-county park, and the Lake District, a single-county park, suggesting that the Government shared the Commission's view of the good work done by their predecessors. Both boards appoint their own staff, hold land, and rely on the constituent counties for their expenditure.

Each of the other eight national parks is administered by a separate main committee of a county council. The county councils provide staff for the work of the committees, hold land needed for park purposes, and meet the expenditure of the committees. The decision whether to spend money or not and what staff to employ

Today the national parks guarantee the chance of escape, albeit
only temporarily, from a captivity more irksome than the Victorians had to endure

rests with the county councils. It remains to be
seen whether the new scheme supported as it is
by new, more powerful county councils and far
better financial arrangements will at last give
imaginative effect in all the national parks to the
purposes for which they have been designated.

A new instrument, the 'national park plan',
clarifies the ways in which the park authorities
determine to do their work. Part of the agreement between the County Councils Association and the Countryside Commission, it was
introduced by the 1972 Act. Every national park
committee and board was required to publish
within three years of 1 April 1974 a national park
plan bringing together its policies for the per-
formance of its functions in the park and relating
them to a definite programme of expenditure.
The national park plan will be reinforced by the
structure plan and local plans of the new-style

development plans, which have been progressively introduced since 1968 in order to provide a stimulus, previously lacking, to the positive creation and maintenance of a good environment.

Structure plans, the responsibility of the boards in the Peak District and the Lake District and of the county councils in the other eight parks, will contain statements of conservation and recreation policies which need to be prepared in the context of regional and sub-regional strategies because recreational activities cross county and national park boundaries. Some of the parks are within easy reach of big centres of population and all the parks are being brought within two or three hours' drive from one or another of the metropolitan conurbations of England and Wales by the building of the motorways.

Groups of local planning authorities including those responsible for conurbations therefore need to combine to review their recreational resources in terms of their relative attraction and their capacity and suitability for development.

The Countryside Act, 1968 and the Countryside (Scotland) Act, 1967, recognised that the post-war leisure 'explosion' had made it necessary to cater for informal outdoor recreation on a nationwide basis. Powers and grants for the creation of country parks, picnic areas, facilities for water-based recreation, and associated services for visitors such as car parks, lavatories, shelters, wardens and information centres became available everywhere in the countryside to local authorities, private individuals and non-public bodies including the National Trust and the National Trust for Scotland.

Country parks are parks or pleasure grounds in countryside, usually quite small from 25 to 1,000 acres or so in extent. Their use is often intensive, but it need not be. Country parks and picnic areas are seen as the main means for coping with the great majority of car-borne visitors to the countryside, who do not wish to move far from their cars but do want to travel somewhere and stop a while on day or half-day trips.

Several recently completed studies, for example the Countryside Commission's coastal reports, suggest the need for regional parks. These parks have a high potential for recreation, are much more extensive than country parks and include a multiplicity of land ownerships; they therefore call for co-ordinated planning and management if their potential is to be realised.

The emphasis when the national parks were established was on preservation and accessibility. It was not possible to draw the boundaries to exclude all quarrying, mining and other incongruous uses. Planning control was, and is, the principal means for preventing the introduction of new uses which would damage natural beauty and its enjoyment and for restraining those which do not harmonise with park purposes. In this work the park authorities need the support of the Countryside Commission and of ministers when it comes to a battle to prevent the qualities of the parks from being diminished. The major decisions to permit or refuse mining, quarrying, reservoirs, oil terminals, power stations and super-grid transmission lines, to continue or discontinue military use, and to make roads for through-traffic to cross the parks, are taken by ministers, rarely by Parliament. Some of the day-to-day business of the park authority reaches the Minister on appeal and again his decision is vital, for the sum of relatively minor, sometimes borderline decisions going the right way also makes the difference between the success and failure of the park authority's policies.

Much of the characteristic landscape beauty of the parks is the joint product of man and nature. It depends on the kind of farming being practised, as John Dower emphasised, both the extensive grazing of the higher open land and the more or less intensive grazing, mowing or cropping of the lower enclosed land. Maintenance of efficient farming in the parks has remained one of the aims of national park policy. Dower certainly expected change and so did the Hobhouse Committee, but they could not have anticipated the scale and rate of change made possible since the late 1950s by agricultural improvement grants, new machinery and new chemicals on the one hand, and by the emergence of forestry syndicates to take advantage of forestry grants and tax concessions on the other.

The use of land for agriculture and forestry, including afforestation, is not 'development' so it cannot be controlled under planning law. In 1961 the strength of public feeling at what seemed to be a threat of extensive conifer planting in Exmoor and Dartmoor led to the negotiation of a voluntary scheme between the Timber Growers' Organisation, the Country Landowners' Association, the Forestry Commission and the National Parks Commission. This was designed to secure the same consultation of park planning authorities on the purchase and planting of open land for private afforestation as was already operating with the Forestry Commission. It depended, of course, on the prospective planter being willing not to exercise his legal right to plant when the park authority sustained objection. Both sides have made concessions and employed landscape architects to try to resolve differences between amenity and economics, but there have been one or two hard cases in nearly every national park. Several park authorities, the Countryside Commission and park enthusiasts would prefer the introduction of straightforward planning control.

In Exmoor, studies of the possibilities for afforestation on open moorland on the one hand, and for restocking in existing woods on the other, revealed a hard core of 'critical amenity areas', stretches of open country and old woods, the conservation of which was critical to the

maintenance of Exmoor's traditional character. They also showed it was possible to identify sites for productive forestry, provided regard was had to the intimate landscape of the park and care was taken over planting designs within them. These studies and similar surveys in other national parks have provided the basis for operating the voluntary scheme, which applies only to open country. Tree preservation orders prevent the felling of existing woods but regeneration or planting is needed to perpetuate them; several park authorities have therefore purchased woods to manage them for amenity, notably Exmoor and the Peak District.

The loss of open country by enclosure and agricultural improvement has proved a far more difficult problem, particularly in Exmoor, about three-quarters of which is now more or less intensively farmed. Dartmoor and the North York Moors are also affected in this way. Apart from land owned by the National Trust or purchased by the county council, retention of these critical amenity areas depends mainly on a good understanding which was reached in 1969 between the park authorities and farmers and landowners.

Suitability of the land for public access offers a solution in some cases, albeit only a partial one. Since 1968 the owners and occupiers of open country have been able to covenant by access agreement with the park authority not to fence or plough or otherwise improve their land agriculturally so that it ceases to be rough grazing and legally 'open country'—on which the public may roam away from roads and paths. In return they receive an annual payment. A warden service is provided by the park authority to serve as a link between farmers and visitors, and to secure compliance with by-laws on the access land and on the approaches to it.

But the perpetuation of a particular kind of ground cover, because it is critical for the character of the landscape and its enjoyment, often requires more management than just the grazing of sheep and cattle on it. It requires controlled burning of heather for example, or skilled silvicultural treatment of old woods. Legislation is needed and has been proposed by the Countryside Commission to enable park authorities to make 'landscape agreements', with payment to the farmers and landowners for managing such areas. Landscape agreements would preserve the appearance of critical amenity areas, or introduce designed change in them. If public access is also required on the same land the two forms of agreement would run together. Until there is legislation farmers and landowners who do co-operate in maintaining critical amenity areas are likely to be out of pocket. If they get fed up and want to improve their land or sell it, purchase by the park authority remains the chief solution. But the national park authorities have no power in the last resort to purchase heather moorland and other open country compulsorily in order simply to preserve it as beautiful scenery.

Freedom to wander at will in open country is an essential purpose of the national parks. Much depends on the friendly understanding of the owners and farmers of the uncultivated mountains, moors and coasts. As the numbers of visitors continue to grow they need more formal access arrangements and strong warden services. The preparation of the first national park plans will, no doubt, be the occasion for a fresh look at the whole question.

Energy conservation – new problem, old pastime – remains a favourite national park 'activity'

Chapter 1

DARTMOOR

Sylvia Sayer

AREA: *365 square miles (91,300ha)*
ALTITUDE: *98 – 2,038ft (30 – 621m)*
 High Willhays 2,038ft (621m)
 Yes Tor 2,030oft (619m)
 Hangingstone Hill 1,983ft (604m)
ADMINISTRATION: *The Dartmoor National Park Committee of the Devon County Council has 21 members, of whom 14 are appointed by the County Council; 11 represent the County Council and 1 each the District Councils of South Hams, Teignbridge, and West Devon. 7 members are appointed by the Secretary of State for the Environment.*
POPULATION: *28,400. Ashburton, 3,495; Buckfastleigh, 2,657; Moretonhampstead, 1,541; Chagford, 1,346.*
COMMUNICATIONS: *There are main line stations close to the north, east and south of the park at Exeter, Newton Abbot, Totnes and Plymouth.*
 By road Exeter to Moretonhampstead is 13 miles, to Chagford 18 miles; Newton Abbot – Ashburton 7 miles; Totnes – Buckfastleigh 8 miles; Plymouth

– Princetown 15 miles.
 Bus services run along the A38 (3 hourly) and the A30; from Torquay to Plymouth and Buckfastleigh, Newton Abbot to Moretonhampstead, and Plymouth to Tavistock. Small bus companies operate services from Newton Abbot to Widecombe and from Tavistock to Okehampton.
VIEWPOINTS *with or near car parks:*
Bellever Tor (SX 645764)
Gibbet Hill (SX 505812)
Haytor Rocks (SX 758771)
Hound Tor (SX 744791)
Staple Tor (SX 543760)
Whitchurch Common (SX 529751)
NATIONAL PARK INFORMATION CENTRE:
Two Bridges (caravan). Near Two Bridges Hotel; tel Princetown 253 (SX 608750)
OTHER VISITOR CENTRES, MUSEUMS:
Sticklepath. Finch Foundry Museum (SX 643940)
NATIONAL PARK OFFICER, *County Hall, Exeter, Devon EX2 4QD*

The great granite mass of Dartmoor dominates Britain's south-western peninsula, and together with the smaller outcrops of Bodmin Moor and west Cornwall, forms its mighty backbone. Dartmoor's special atmosphere and character derive not only from the dramatic uprising of its high bare hills and rocky tors above the snug cultivated farmland of rural Devon but also from the haunting influence of its prehistoric past. The Celtic survivors ('Wealas') of Dart-

moor's prehistoric population left their traces in some place-names (eg Wallabrook, Wellsfoot Island), but most of the prehistoric remains to be found far and wide on the moor are of much earlier date, and they endow it with a feeling of timelessness, a feeling that here the past and present are one.

A newcomer to Dartmoor with no particular knowledge of its geology might well suppose that the great rock masses of its tors had existed

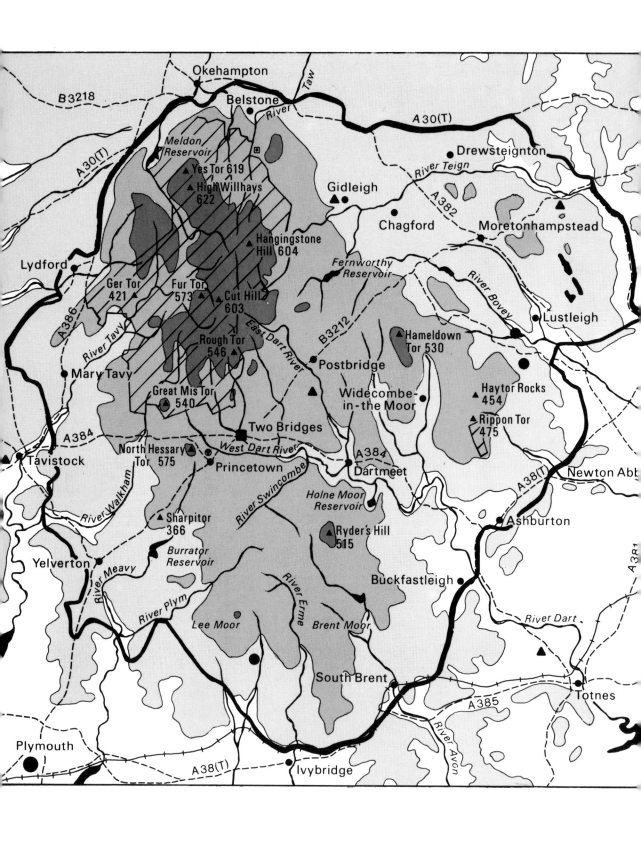

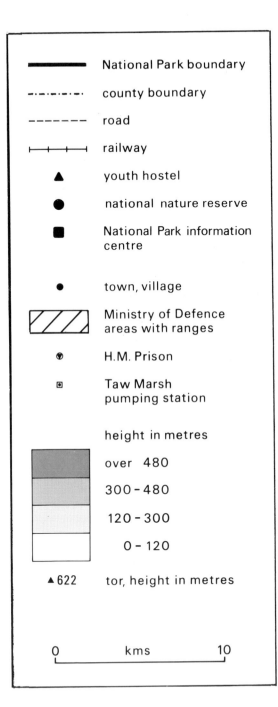

National Park boundary

county boundary

road

railway

▲   youth hostel

●   national nature reserve

■   National Park information centre

•   town, village

Ministry of Defence areas with ranges

H.M. Prison

Taw Marsh pumping station

height in metres

over 480

300 - 480

120 - 300

0 - 120

▲ 622   tor, height in metres

0   kms   10

in their present visible form and solidity from the first stages of our West Country's emergence from the receding primeval seas. But in fact there were once no tors visible at all; a great thickness of shales, grits and limestone—the Devonian and Carboniferous beds of country rock, deposited as sediment when Devon lay under the sea—covered the whole Dartmoor area more than 290 million years ago.

Then came the vast earthquake disturbances that rammed what were to be Devon and Cornwall against the older rock structure of Wales, crumpling and cracking the roof of country rock, and accompanied by an upboiling of molten magma from the earth's depths. This thrust into the pressurised folds and by its enormous heat baked the broken rock cover; boiling fluids, gases and steam intruded into the granite and its surrounding rock and created its coveted minerals—tin, copper, zinc, lead, iron, china clay.

In time the broken cover eroded away, leaving the harder granite cores of the cooled magma piercing the Dartmoor sky. These were the tors, and at first they were much higher than they are today. Now the highest tor on Dartmoor (High Willhays) is just over 2,000ft above sea-level, but millions of years of weathering have slowly reduced and rounded all the rock masses, and it is estimated that as much as 650ft of the granite may have been lost by erosion since it was first uncovered.

Primeval Dartmoor endured further submergences and earth movements which tilted the whole granite mass towards the east and south. The final tilting determined the flow of the Dartmoor rivers and also accounts for the difference in height between northern and southern Dartmoor. By now the essential Dartmoor, which was to mean so much to so many, was already in being.

One can still see the flow of the molten magma petrified in the coarser granites of the

The view from Combestone Tor is typical of much of Dartmoor,
displaying the bleak majesty of a land unchanged for centuries

moor—the Tor or Giant granite as it is called. Surrounding the whole Dartmoor mass is the 'metamorphic aureole', the tilted Devonian and Carboniferous rock baked out of its original character by the first great upheaval.

The granite is mainly composed of three different minerals—quartz, felspar and mica or biotite—but there are other intrusions, and endless variations of colour and composition are played on this geological theme, including the outcrops of red granite on southern Dartmoor once much fancied by wealthy Victorians for mantelpieces and tombstones.

The tors themselves rise in massive rock-piles, weathered and naturally jointed, above Dart-moor's undulating highland. Their strange block-like formation is unique to Dartmoor and the Cornish moors, and is totally unlike the crags and mountain peaks of northern Britain and Wales. Although the south-western peninsula escaped being covered with ice during the several Ice Ages, their savage frosts attacked the joints in the tor blocks, breaking down the granite and pushing the loose material down the slopes. These deposits of granite boulders fanning down the hillsides are the Dartmoor 'clitters'—not easy to climb over, as the smaller rocks often move and can throw the unwary.

Weathering has done strange things to the tors. It has sometimes left huge loose boulders poised on rocky pivots, so that these boulders— the logan or 'logging' stones—could be rocked at the touch of a hand. (Or, as was solemnly claimed for the Rugglestone logan at Widecombe, only at the touch of the church key.) It also produced another curiosity, the natural rock basins which can be found on many tor summits. The most famous of these is Mis Tor Pan, known to the ancients as The Devil's Frying Pan, on top of one of the summit stacks of Great Mis Tor. This is also one of the historic bondstones or boundary marks of the central Dartmoor Forest (which is not a forest at all, but an ancient royal hunting ground still owned by the Prince of Wales), and was mentioned as such in a deed of Isabella de Fortibus, Countess of Devon, as long ago as 1291, and again in a survey of 1609 as 'a rock called Mistorrpan'. It survived undamaged until April 1960. Then some nameless barbarian must have taken an iron bar to it: an arched section of its rim was levered off and fell at the foot of the stack. Isabella de Fortibus, a proud and powerful character, would surely have known how to deal with this destroyer.

Dartmoor's climate has been much warmer than it is now, and about 5000 BC the heath land and birch forests gave way to mixed woodlands of oak and elm, and peat began to form on the high land. The natural moorland soil has much peat in it even today, producing the moor's characteristic vegetation of tough grasses, mosses, rushes, heather and furze, bracken and whortleberry, which breathe out the clean and heady freshness of wild country—a miracle of primitive survival in this much-polluted island. The deeper 'blanket bog' peat is found in great fissured plateaux on northern Dartmoor and on some of its southern high land, where it is still forming.

Peat was for centuries a staple Dartmoor fuel, and peat diggers have found trunks and branches of ancient blackened bog oak embedded below the surface of their cuttings. The widespread primeval oakwoods have long disappeared from the higher moor, though three tenacious and famous remnants still cling deep-rooted to the rocky valleys of the upper West Dart (Wistman's Wood), the upper West Okement (Black Tor Beare) and the upper Erme (Piles Wood), and are scheduled for protection by the Nature Conservancy.

Today the moor's climate is one of high rainfall—80in or more in some areas—and frequent mists, and its winters are formidable, often producing near-arctic conditions with snow-filled lanes and deep moorland drifts. Sometimes a wet spell followed immediately by extreme cold has a lethal effect on the animals wintered on the moor; their wet coats become an armourplating of ice, and their frozen corpses are found in harrowing numbers on the high land. But Dartmoor's summer weather can be gloriously hot and sunny, with quivering heat mirages hovering above its long horizons. Its droughts also can be prolonged, so that as the moorland reservoirs empty long-drowned roads and little stone bridges emerge again into the light of day and the cry of 'water shortage' is raised in the surrounding towns. Dartmoor is a land of contrasts and extremes—beautiful, cruel, inspiring, unpredictable, spell-binding. Its spell is unique.

The first Dartmoor farmers were the Neolithic or New Stone Age people, who had learned the mysteries of cattle rearing, seed planting and cultivation. They made clearings in the woodland and hunted birds and beasts with arrows tipped with leaf-shaped flint heads. These Neolithic people kept cattle, sheep and pigs, but not the Dartmoor pony; horses were not brought to Britain before the Bronze Age (1900 BC), but since then the famous hardy ponies have continued to survive on the moor, and the Dartmoor National Park Committee adopted a stylised symbol of the Dartmoor pony as the national park sign or badge.

By far the greatest number of prehistoric dwellings and monuments on the moor are those of the Bronze Age people who migrated to it from Europe. But not many bronze objects have been found on Dartmoor; this latest wave of settlers evidently continued to use flint—brought from outside the moor as there is no natural flint there—to make their beautifully worked barbed-and-tanged arrowheads, scrapers, knives and borers. These are still quite plentiful on Dartmoor, if you know where and how to look.

The Bronze Age people buried their dead doubled up or cremated in stone chests (kists) covered with a mound of earth or stone; these, together with their ceremonial stone circles and avenues of standing stones, their round hut circles and 'pounds'—stone enclosures built to surround their huts and tethered animals and to keep out the wolves and other wild beasts—are part of the character and fascination of Dartmoor.

There is some evidence that the prehistoric people had a sense of fun. I found near the great menhir on Langstone Moor a flint pebble which had been worked for use as a scraper, but still retained much of its natural pale grey outer surface. It had the shape of a bird's or small mammal's head, and a dark 'eye' had been carefully and deliberately chiselled into the natural surface to make the resemblance complete. Was this done to amuse some much-loved child about 4,000 years ago? That stone seemed to bring the prehistoric Dartmoor dwellers very close as I stood on the lonely moor with it in my hand.

The groups of Celtic people who began arriving on Dartmoor from France and Belgium in the fifth century BC also farmed and lived in round stone huts, but they had mastered the mysteries of iron smelting; a hut near Kes Tor (Chagford) has been identified as an iron worker's, possessing a furnace and pit as well as sleeping quarters.

But with this further advance towards civilisation came civilisation's curse—the fear of attack, the knowledge that others might covet one's land and possessions. Dartmoor became ringed with hill forts, massive earthworks on the border crests, often with complicated systems of defensive banks and ditches. Wooston Castle, high above the Teign, is one such. Unfortunately it is now covered with bristling conifers, so that the skill of its planning is hard to see and appreciate.

The Romans allowed the native tribes (the Dumnonii) to pursue their farming way of life on the moor unmolested. No doubt the Roman rulers kept a possessive hand on the tin trade in the South West, but this was centred mainly in Cornwall; there is no definite evidence of tin working on Dartmoor until early medieval times.

The inscribed Celtic memorial stones at Sourton Down (near Okehampton) and at Sticklepath, Buckland Monachorum and Tavistock, are relics of Roman influence. The tall Sourton stone, now passed unnoticed by thousands of speeding motorists on the A30 trunk road, was dedicated to a Celtic prince, Audetus. At some time an attempt was made to fashion it into a cross, but not very successfully; its little stumpy arms are so rudimentary as to be only just able to declare their Christian intention.

Christianity reached Dartmoor in Celtic times, and some of the moor's village churches are dedicated to Celtic saints. In other ways too the Christian faith left indelible marks on Dartmoor. The Sourton cross is only one of a great many ancient granite crosses which still mark trackways or boundaries on the upland. The monks of the three abbeys of Tavistock, Buckland and Buckfast, which, with Plympton Priory, ringed Dartmoor and influenced its history for many centuries, were no doubt responsible for erecting most of the crosses. They had to make many journeys across the moor not only to visit each other but to oversee the stewardship of their land and flocks—occasionally with argument and feuding, as old records drily reveal. Other traders in wool and tin also used these ancient ways, as did the moor-dwellers of medieval times who had to carry their dead many miles to Lydford for burial.

Today traces of these trackways—the Abbot's Way, the Lich Way, the King Way and many others—may still be followed across the high moor, fording its rivers and streams. They are a challenge and delight to adventurous walkers and riders, but their whole lengths should not be attempted when a Dartmoor mist is threatening or when there is snow on the heights.

The Saxon invaders who pushed their way up on to Dartmoor early in the eighth century AD made their clearings first in the more sheltered valleys, founding settlements that continue as hamlets and villages today. Other Saxon villages on the higher moor, still lived in until medieval times, were deserted in the twelfth or thirteenth centuries. These deserted villages—at Houndtor, Blackaton, Challacombe and Okehampton Park—somehow escaped recognition and dating until quite recently; the oblong foundations of their huts, almost buried beneath whortleberry and heather, did not declare their antiquity as clearly as the round walls of the prehistoric hut circles. They are now seen as valuable survivals, evidence of the continuity and variety of life on Dartmoor through the centuries. But why were they abandoned, more than 600 years ago? Was the cause a succession of bad winters, or cruel visitations of plague or of predatory neighbours? We shall probably never know.

One village that has most notably survived from Saxon times is Lydford—the 'capital of Dartmoor', with its deep river gorge (fortunately owned by the National Trust), its castle, where offenders against the royal hunting laws and the tinners' autocratic rule were harshly

judged, its ninth-century earth walls and its Saxon street pattern. In the tenth and eleventh centuries it also had a mint, making silver pennies for the King. It faced a terrifying invasion in AD 997 when the Danes, after burning Tavistock Abbey, tried unsuccessfully to storm Lydford's defences. This is the most interesting village on Dartmoor, far more so than beautiful but commercialised Widecombe. It is a matter for grief that the planners have allowed and are still allowing a fungus of characterless modern bungalows to grow around its perimeter. This is surely one village at least where no further building ought to be permitted.

Dartmoor's wild uplands were valued even before the Norman Conquest as a royal hunting ground or 'forest', rich in game—deer, boar, badger, fox, hare and wolf. These were officially forbidden to the peasantry, but they too used the moor as a summer grazing ground, and a Dartmoor commoner's rights stretch back for centuries. The Normans marked out the forest bounds but left the moormen's rights undisturbed. With the passage of time these rights have inevitably become less clearly defined or effectively supervised and there are now many dubious 'commoners' and much over-stocking, which new legislation must endeavour to correct. Dartmoor being Dartmoor, the reformers are faced with a particular knotty task.

In 1336 or 1337 Edward III created his son the Black Prince Duke of Cornwall, granting him at the same time the castle and manor of Lydford and the Chase of Dartmoor; and from that time Dartmoor Forest or Chase has belonged to the Duchy of Cornwall, vested in the Prince of Wales when there is one living, and at other times in the custody of the Crown. There can be no doubt that on balance this royal ownership has protected Dartmoor, and that without it the South West's last great wilderness would have been even more ruthlessly exploited.

But the Duchy itself has not been blameless in

23

Dartmoor ponies, for many the very essence of the moor,
enjoy the fitful sunshine of a blustery day, while in the background
Haytor watches impassively

the past. In the eighteenth and nineteenth centuries it encouraged wholesale enclosure of the open moorland far in excess of the traditional eight-acre plot, seriously curtailing the commoners' rights and setting an example which adjacent lords of manors hastened to follow. The legacy of this has been the planting by the Forestry Commission and others of thousands of acres of these vast stone-walled 'newtakes' with blankets of conifers, or their recent partition by farmers with miles of barbed wire. Yet this is land which should still by right be open common, and would be had past commoners known how to fight such huge enclosures.

It was primarily to combat the unlawful enclosure of common land that the Dartmoor Preservation Association was founded in 1883. The Association now has to fight even more serious threats, but today its efforts are backed whole-heartedly by the Duchy which uses its great influence on the side of conservation. In 1970 the Prince's Council entered the lists of the objectors against the indefensible Swincombe reservoir scheme, which would have blighted a large area of central Dartmoor. The reservoir Bill was most properly rejected by Parliament.

Tin mining on Dartmoor, now defunct, flourished between the twelfth and seventeenth centuries, but after that declined, with a relatively short-lived revival in Victorian times. The tinners have left widespread evidence of their work on the Dartmoor landscape. Almost every river valley has its tumbled heaps of rock spoil, its ancient leat channels and ruined blowing-houses, where the earlier miners (known to their successors as 'the old men') smelted the ore and cast it into blocks, which were laboriously transported by packhorse to the stannary towns of Ashburton, Chagford, Plympton and Tavistock. Because these workings were on the primitive scale of manual labour and were not subject to the earth-moving might of the machinery that obliterates whole landscapes today, nature has been able to heal and cover them, and they have become assimilated again into the wild Dartmoor scene.

Other minerals—copper, lead, iron—were also mined in the nineteenth century, mainly on the Dartmoor borderland, but not extensively or for long. It would be a very different matter were modern mineral prospectors to try to exploit what may be left of the Dartmoor ores. This would mean widespread and massive destruction, totally unacceptable in any national park or 'area of outstanding natural beauty', and any such proposals would be fought to the utmost. The china clay mining on southern Dartmoor, which began on a small scale early in the last century, demonstrates the results of industrial escalation; it is now carried on with enormous destructiveness, and the giant china clay companies have just obtained ministerial consent for massive further expansion.

Dartmoor's native industry is hill farming and stock rearing. Traditional Dartmoor farming—the careful cultivation of the little sheltered fields near the farm, the summer grazing of cattle and sheep on the moor, the animals wintered on the farms and lowlands—not only conserved the land and protected the landscape but also went hand in hand with the unwritten right of people, whether visitors or inhabitants, to wander freely as they had done for thousands of years. Even as late as the 1950s this 'de facto' right was rarely challenged. But farming practices on Dartmoor, as everywhere else, are changing fast, and with it the farmer's attitude to walkers on the moor. There are fewer of the traditional farmers now, and many more newcomers, often wealthy, who resent the ancient custom of free access to the moorland. Unfortunately they are able to take advantage of government grants that encourage the fencing and ploughing of open country, and care little for the ancient monuments that are all too often destroyed in the process. Sheep and cattle are now wintered in great numbers on the moor, and after a spell of hard weather the corpses of sheep confront the walker in grisly profusion. Hay is taken to the hordes of cattle by heavy tractors and trailers which rut and mash the wet moorland and the old green trackways. This is modern 'economic' farming, but it is exacting a heavy price from the national park.

Most taxpayers would willingly contribute financial help for upland farmers to return to the old careful husbandry that suited and respected the land, its animals, its wildlife, its prehistoric treasures and its ancient freedoms. This message has been put to ministers over and over again, with urgency, but so far without success.

Although almost every Dartmoor farm now has one or two large white corrugated asbestos buildings dominating the farmyard and the surrounding landscape, many very beautiful old granite farmhouses still flourish, and in some villages—North Bovey for example—there is still plenty of thatch. All the oldest Dartmoor farmhouses were built on the immemorial longhouse plan, easily recognisable in some of them even today. For centuries cattle and people entered the long thatched house together by a central cross-passage, the animals then turning one way (usually to the right) into their own living-space with its rough pens and cobbled floor draining out into the farmyard, and the people turning left through a door into the rush-floored chamber, where a peat fire burned day and night on a huge stone hearth hung with iron cooking pots and flanked with a wooden settle. The family and farm workers sat on wooden benches, eating together at a long trestle table; at night the farmer and his family slept in the one upper room, reached by a winding stone stair above the cavernous bread oven. The farm boys slept in the loft above the cattle, and no doubt were thankful for their steamy warmth.

Today these simple, beautiful old Dartmoor farmhouses, provided with additional living space and all mod cons including electricity, are immensely sought after and fetch prices which would cause their first inhabitants to think (not entirely without reason) that the world had gone mad.

The rough, hard Dartmoor way of life continued virtually unchanged for many centuries. Until the end of the eighteenth century, the tracks across the moor were too primitive for wheeled vehicles, and goods were transported as of old by strings of pack ponies or donkeys. Communication was difficult; even at Bridford, on Dartmoor's edge, they did not learn of the death of King George III until three weeks after the event!

But the Dartmoor that ground its own corn, brewed its own cider, made its own boots and clothes, forged its own tools and farm implements, had already begun to disappear. Soon came the moneyed 'improver' with his short-lived dreams of converting the rocky moorland into rich acres of corn and flax; Sir Thomas Tyrwhitt built Princetown and persuaded the Government to build the prison there—where, owing to the lie of the land, the climate is the worst and wettest in Devon. Fired by the improvement mania, several other would-be captains of industry experimented with the commercial production of peat, naphtha, ice and even gunpowder from the moor, but all failed. The Dartmoor adage 'You scratch my back and I'll scratch your pocket' sums up the native moorman's dour opinion of these enterprises.

By the 1870s the War Department had begun to establish a footing on northern Dartmoor, though for many years the firing area was relatively small and it was not until 1948 that the military authorities (after a farcical public inquiry) were given Government permission to use almost the whole northern half of Dartmoor for live ammunition training and thousands more acres of southern Dartmoor for 'damaging training but without live ammunition'.

When the National Parks and Access to the Countryside Act was passed in 1949 and Dartmoor's designation as a national park followed in 1951, those who loved the moor dared to hope that the new national park's 365 square miles—200 of them moorland, the rest woodland or cultivated land—might at last be effectively protected. Mr Harold Macmillan told Parliament in 1952 that in national parks the claims of amenity and access were to be given top priority, and for a short time this seemed believable: surely everyone could see that Dartmoor had already suffered more than a reasonable share of encroachment on its natural beauty —the prison, the enclosures, the military, china clay mining, many reservoirs, Forestry Commission plantations blanketing large parts of the central moor; surely now there would be an end to all this creeping appropriation; surely now wild Dartmoor was safe?

But wild Dartmoor is still anything but safe. No honest description of this national park can ignore this unhappy fact. Dartmoor's natural

The ancient clapper bridge at Dartmeet, where the East and West Dart meet, was partially destroyed in 1826 but has since been repaired. Clapper bridges are made of unwrought granite slabs and are thought to have been constructed in the thirteenth and fourteenth centuries, although Teignhead Farm boasts an unusual eighteenth-century example

character has actually suffered more erosion and serious threat since its designation as a national park than ever before. Since designation it has had imposed upon it: the 750ft television mast on Hessary Tor; the military construction of a vast network of roads on northern Dartmoor bringing hordes of cars into its wildest area; the stepping-up of military activities generally, plus low flying jet aircraft and helicopters; the Taw Marsh pumping station; commercial afforestation of the moor by private forestry syndicates combined with widespread felling of natural valley woodlands; the new fencing and ploughing of open moorland ('improvement' again); the spreading growth of substandard speculative building in the villages; the china clay mining expansion; the particularly indefensible Meldon reservoir; the rising and ineffectively controlled tide of motor vehicles—cars, lorries, coaches, mobile canteens, caravans—jamming the ancient lanes and trespassing on to the open moorland. In the 'threat' pipeline are more major waterworks, and an Okehampton bypass totally destructive of rare and splendid landscape. The metal mining speculators hover just around the corner.

The main reasons for this dismal situation are first, that no British government has ever yet taken the protection of national parks sufficiently seriously, or provided the National Parks Commission (now the Countryside Commission) with enough powers or money, and secondly that most national parks—the Peak and the Lakes excepted—are still subject to county council control. Dartmoor has never yet been a national park in anything but name. It is a county council park, run by a county council committee with only a small proportion of nationally appointed members. Dartmoor must therefore continue to take its chance at the hands of local interests, and until there is a top-level change of policy and of legislation it is hard to feel much optimism about its future.

The Dartmoor National Park is ringed by cities and towns, some large, all expanding. Very naturally their inhabitants drive their cars in ever-greater numbers up to Dartmoor for a day's touring or picnicking or a weekend's camping. Added to the inevitable growth in population with its subsequent increase in traffic, the M5 motorway when complete will greatly augment the number of long-distance day visitors to Dartmoor. The county planning officer estimates that then 'nearly 95,000 people could be expected to visit Dartmoor on peak days'.

The Devon County Council's Dartmoor National Park Committee has produced a policy plan for the national park which is good in principle, with proposals for creating motorless zones and for grappling with traffic problems, but the implementation of the plan is proceeding so slowly that effective safeguards are unlikely to be operating before the situation reaches near-chaos.

Motorists must of course come to Dartmoor, but if they are not to ruin it (and their own and others' enjoyment of it) they must face increasing control and prohibition—simply because of the weight of their own numbers. There will have to be some inner areas of the park where no cars may enter at all; some lanes prohibited to motor vehicles but open to cyclists and horse-drawn vehicles; a system of one-way routes; embargoes on vehicles over a certain size and width; and large, perimeter, car parks where people will leave their cars and then use a system of cheap minibus transport worked out to allow whole days spent walking, riding, fishing or picnicking on the moor. The accent should increasingly be on public transport and fewer private cars. The defunct rail services Plymouth-Yelverton-Tavistock and Exeter-Okehampton-Tavistock should be brought back into use. They could play a most important part in bringing people within walking or cycling distance of the moorland, and would be well patronised once the private car was brought under more stringent control.

Why is wild country worth saving? Why does Dartmoor need special protection?

The answer must lie within people themselves, something to be felt rather than analysed. Some regard Dartmoor simply as a barren waste, while others feel the magic of the place, perceiving that on Dartmoor's wild upland is written the history of the British race, and experiencing a sense of liberation and renewal whenever they set foot on it. They love its space and solitude, and the sound of the rivers that are Dartmoor itself with their lovely Celtic names—Dart, Tavy, Avon, Meavy, Ockment, Teign—rushing and cascading over their bouldered beds.

Certainly wild country can be stern and austere and very testing, soaking the adventurous walker or rider to the skin, or freezing him to the marrow, reducing life almost to its barest elements. But something in human beings responds to this primeval toughness, and having surmounted it, feels enormously proud and benefitted by the experience.

National parks are not just a nice but slightly unnecessary luxury for a fortunate few. They are a vital provision for a very real human need. Far from being barren or unproductive, our wild uplands provide the most valuable products of all—the products of health and happiness—at a time when such simple and uncomplicated benefits are in ever-shorter supply.

What is desperately needed is that the value of wilderness should be fully understood and legislated for, while there is still some wilderness left to save. If this can be achieved—but only if it can be achieved—wild Dartmoor will survive.

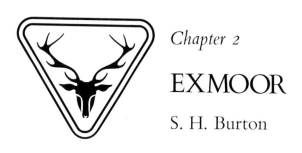

Chapter 2

EXMOOR

S. H. Burton

AREA: *265 square miles (68,632ha)*
ALTITUDE: *0 – 1,704ft (0 – 520m)*
     Dunkery Beacon 1,704ft (520m)
     Five Barrows 1,617ft (480m)
     Chains Barrow 1,599ft (477m)
ADMINISTRATION: *The Exmoor National Park Committee, a separate committee of the Somerset County Council, has 21 members of whom 14 are appointed by the County Council; 8 represent Somerset County Council, 4 Devon County Council and 1 each the District Councils of West Somerset and North Devon. 7 members are appointed by the Secretary of State for the Environment.*
POPULATION: *14,400. Lynton and Lynmouth, 1,981; Dulverton, 1,392; Porlock, 1,307; Dunster, 958.*
COMMUNICATIONS: *There are rail services to Bridgwater, Taunton, Exeter and Barnstaple near the park. A private company is hoping to re-open the Taunton to Minehead line.*

   By road Bridgwater to Dunster is 25 miles; Taunton – Dunster 22 miles; Exeter – Dulverton 27 miles; Barnstaple – Lynton 17 miles.

   Within the park bus services are scanty. Dulverton has bus links with Minehead and Bampton. Minehead is linked with Porlock and Porlock Weir, and from May to September with Lynmouth.
VIEWPOINTS *with or near car parks:*
Chains Barrow (SS 735419)
Dunkery Beacon (SS 891416)
North Hill (SS 943475)
Quarme Hill (SS 934370)
Winsford Hill (SS 877343)
Yenworthy Common (SS 808479)
NATIONAL PARK INFORMATION CENTRES:
Combe Martin (caravan). The Beach Car Park; tel Combe Martin 3319 (SS 576474)
Lynton. Lyn and Exmoor Museum, Market Street (SS 720493)
Minehead. Market House, The Parade; tel Minehead 2984 (SS 968462)
NATIONAL PARK INFORMATION OFFICER, *Market House, The Parade, Minehead, Somerset TA24 5NB*

Nowhere else in Britain can greater variety of scene be found than within the comparatively small territory of the Exmoor National Park. In its 170,000 acres lie heather and grass moors, deciduous woodlands and coniferous forests, a high plateau, deep, steep-sided valleys, farm land varying from arable to rough grazing, and dramatic coastal cliffs. Nor do its settlements conform to an easily discernible pattern: lonely farmhouses, tiny hamlets, moorland villages, deserted mining camps, and a few little townships which during the season fleetingly assume a resort-like appearance.

   And if its personality is many sided, its administration for long lacked unity. About two-thirds of Exmoor lies in Somerset and the remainder in Devon; in 1954, when the park came into being, this fact was held to justify the creation of a Somerset National Park Committee, a Devon National Park Committee, and a Joint Advisory Committee to co-ordinate the policies of the other two.

Variety has been stressed. Exmoor is also a secret and elusive place. The visitor who drives from Dulverton to Lynmouth, via Winsford Hill and Simonsbath, will find those adjectives justified by every mile of his journey. Not more than twice between starting and stopping points does the moor reveal itself.

Two essential points must be made: Exmoor can only be glimpsed from a car; and even those who are willing to get out and stretch their legs can see at any one time only one, or at most two, of the many Exmoors that exist.

The interlacing of farm land and moorland must also be realised if the personality of Exmoor is to be understood. The geographical and historical factors involved will be explored later; here, the resultant fact is the issue. The moorland farms depend on their wild 'allotments' as vitally as on their improved 'inbye' fields. Each is an essential element in the agricultural economy. Tongues of reclaimed land thrust deep into the moors. Huge, open grazings are bounded by beech-hedged enclosures. Thus the moor comes and goes: appears and disappears. This is not a 'big wilderness' in the way that most of the other national parks are. The scenic, amenity and agricultural consequences are of the greatest significance. General policies may be conceived, but they require frequent and local modification. Exmoor is not all of a piece. There are many Exmoors within the park boundary, each presenting peculiar problems.

Both native and visitor may well enquire how it was possible to designate this area and to draw its boundaries; and those of us who were concerned in those distant days with the creation of 'The Park' do well to remind ourselves of the factors that had to be faced.

The National Parks and Access to the Countryside Act of 1949 provided that certain areas of Britain should be recognised as being of particular importance to the nation as a whole. That special importance attached to several tracts of wild natural beauty, each characterised by structural, topographical, vegetational and scenic features that gave it individual identity. Defining the boundaries of each park was difficult: defining Exmoor's boundary was necessarily arbitrary. Not merely did 'the moor' shade off imperceptibly into the surrounding countryside, but the various moors within the moor would continue to co-exist within any conceivable and practicable boundary. Only in the north, where cliffs met sea, was it possible to make the park map without much thought—and even there the problem of eastward and westward extensions was acute. Why stop short of Minehead? Why not include Combe Martin? Why that great eastward loop round the Brendons? And if the Brendons were to be in, why not include the Quantocks?

Had it been either possible or desirable to proceed solely by the criterion of character or identity, then logically 'The Forest' would have constituted the park—or the coastal belt—or Dunkery's heather top and cleaving combes—or the southern ridge—or one of the major river systems—or …

Finally, after much thought and with many problems left unsolved, the designated area emerged as a tract of West Somerset and North Devon. Unity within diversity had to be imposed and, owing to several common factors, a park identity—tenuous but discernible—has gradually grown.

Foremost among those common factors is the character of Exmoor people and their way of life. Details about the moorland farming come later, but no description of Exmoor's elusive identity can omit reference to its people. A hard life and a hostile climate, intractable land and family labour coupled with low rewards,

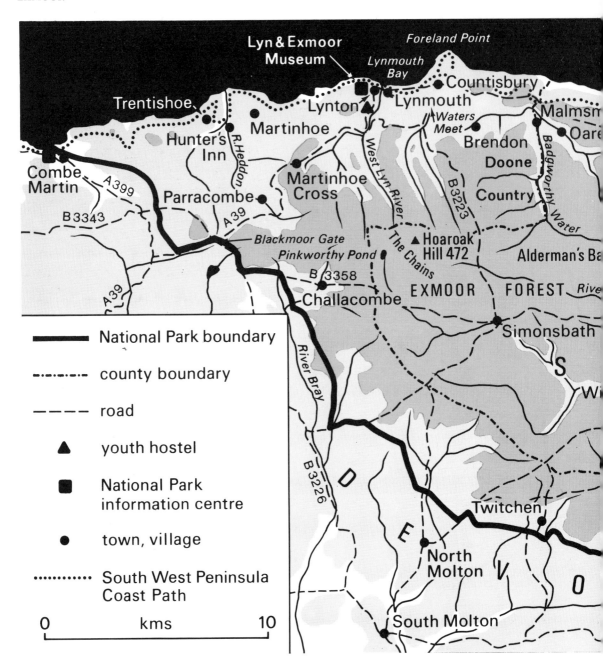

National Park boundary

county boundary

road

▲ youth hostel

■ National Park information centre

● town, village

South West Peninsula Coast Path

0   kms   10

fluctuating government policies and geographical isolation, have produced a special breed. A fierce independence—a great desire to be left alone—has resulted. The villages and little towns share these characteristics. Recent devel-

opments have done much to dilute the isolation, but October's arrival permits the moorland communities to return to their own life: a life in which farmer, villager and townsman still share. The disruption of 'the season' is an

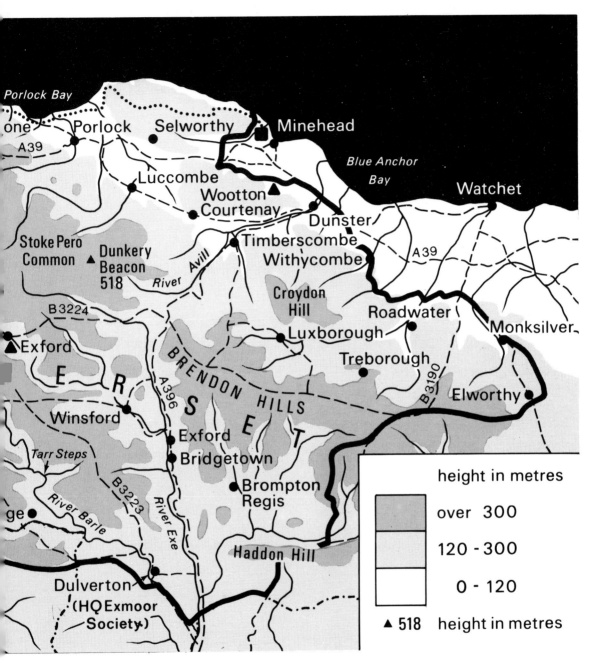

annual aberration. Autumn, winter and spring return Exmoor's inhabitants to their innate ways—to a life, whether in moorland farmstead or village street, that is still dominated by the leaden rain clouds, the persistent mists, the settled warmth of the Indian summer, the fitful glories of March and April, or the venomous blizzards 'up over'. The moor remains the dominant factor in our lives.

Second in importance among the Exmoor

characteristics is the existence of the wild red deer. Apart from the Scottish Highlands, Exmoor is the last secure home of large herds of Britain's biggest and loveliest wild mammal. Here still, as in the prehistoric past, *Cervus elaphus* lives as a free wild creature, thriving on the produce of the moorland farms—their woodland, their rough grazing, their improved pasture, their root and corn crops.

About 800 deer live within the park boundary, and their numbers make some form of control imperative. The herds must be culled if farmer and animal are to co-exist. Again, the agility and power of the stag and the cunning of the hind make impossible any attempt to fence them out. Deer-proof fencing round every Exmoor field would bankrupt the wealthiest estate. Even if it were practicable, however, it would not be done. Hunting the deer is the traditional Exmoor method of control. The farmers and landowners tolerate deer damage in return for the sport: abolish the hunt and you abolish the deer as a *wild* species.

The question of the deer is the most dramatic of several issues symptomatic of Exmoor's character and problems. The outside world is exerting pressures that take little notice of the people's needs. Fewer sheep on the moors, fewer jobs on the farms, fewer people in the villages: more and more visitors, overcrowded summer roads, a sense of exploitation, a slow unwilling acceptance of dependence, an instinctive awareness by the moor dwellers that their lives are being changed by forces that care little for their native ways. Ultimately they take the only course open to them: they adapt.

Unlike the other south-western moorlands, Exmoor is not a granite tract. Apart from a few intrusions of New Red Sandstone (the Vale of Porlock is the most notable example) Devonian rock dominates the scene, band after band of its local varieties unfolding in sequence from north to south until the moor ends where the Devonian system dips under the Culm Measures. No two experts seem able to agree about the origin and subsequent history of this complex structure, but its topographical and agricultural consequences are readily described.

The centre of Exmoor is dominated by a high plateau, its rolling surface undulating very gradually. A few eminences—such as Chains Barrow (1,599ft)—break through the pattern, but the overall impression is of uniformity, both in altitude and vegetation.

In the north, the plateau is cut through by deep valleys down which little streams rush towards the Bristol Channel, all these northern waters finding their way to the sea at Lynmouth. A magnificent bastion of hog's-back cliffs extends from Combe Martin in the west to Minehead in the east; the only considerable break in this cliff wall occurring on the shores of Porlock Bay.

In the south, the moor's two chief rivers rise out of the grass moorland. The Barle and the Exe are born only two miles apart, but diverging courses make them strangers to each other until the Exe captures the Barle south of Dulverton.

East of the moorland plateau—the heart of which is picturesquely and accurately known as The Chains—heather moor is dominant. Dunkery (1,704ft), Winsford Hill (1,399ft) and the Commons of the two Ansteys are the most notable of these heather-clad heights, divided from each other by deep and heavily wooded valleys.

Between the eastern heather moor and the western grass, the swampy middle moor imposes a barrier that—as yet—keeps this area comparatively free of visitors. Some of Exmoor's most solitary walking may be found along the Lark Barrow-Tom's Hill-Badgworthy routes.

Above the 1,300ft contour line the soil is wet and peaty. Drainage is also very poor, for a continuous and impermeable iron pan underlies the thin, acid soil. On lower ground, there is a good topsoil resting on shale. Here drainage is no problem, but even the good soil areas are deficient in lime and require heavy dressings.

Rock does not freely outcrop on Exmoor: a fact that helps to account for the comparative scarceness of megalithic monuments. Apart from the famous Longstone, near Chapman Barrows on the western moor, the stone prehistoric remains—the circle on Withypool Hill, for example, or the quadrilateral on Furzehill Common—are unimpressive, judged either by the size or the number of their component parts. Yet it is remarkable that they are there at all. Finding and transporting the stones must have been a tremendous labour for the Beaker Folk or early Bronze Age men who set them up for purposes at which we can but guess.

In the later Bronze Age (down to about 500 BC) climatic conditions on Exmoor were more favourable to human habitation of the higher moorland combes than they have ever been since. The comparative density of moorland settlement in that period is indicated by the number of round barrows which mark the skylines of the National Park. Particularly fine are the barrow clusters at Five Barrows and Chapman Barrows, while notable individual examples occur on the Brendons. Funereal ostentation on this scale indicates a labour force and an organisation capable of expressing the cultural values of a thriving community.

The climatic deterioration which drove Bronze Age man off the moorland top was accompanied by infiltration of Exmoor by Iron Age immigrants. For perhaps 200 years the intermingling of the older and the newer cultures appears to have proceeded peacefully, though there seems little doubt that the newcomers built their simple univallate 'castles' as soon as they arrived.

In about 300 BC, however, a more aggressive invader arrived. Belgic tribes approached the Exmoor region, and it seems likely that the comparatively ambitious multivallate 'castles' on the perimeters of the moor were hastily thrown up by the Dumnonii as a defence against these vigorous newcomers.

The Claudian invasion of Britain in AD 43 checked the expansive activities of the Belgic peoples. Consequently, the Dumnonii were still in secure occupation of such of Exmoor as they wanted when the Romans arrived in this isolated and remote area. There is no evidence to suggest that the 'natives' gave the Romans any trouble or that Exmoor's bleak and inhospitable interior was of the slightest interest either to the conquerors or to the indigenous dwellers on its fringes. At Old Burrow and Martinhoe the Romans established small garrisons and signalling stations, the purpose of which was to guard against sea-borne raids by the Silures of South Wales rather than to police the Dumnonii.

The pattern established once the Bronze Age ended was thus perpetuated in Roman times. It was to persist throughout the Dark Ages, Saxon and Norman England, and right down to the nineteenth century. The central lands of Exmoor were virtually uninhabited: the fringes and the valleys were sparsely and intermittently settled. Saxon place names trace the progress of settlement between AD 690 and 710 and it is noteworthy that there are only two such names (Pinkworthy and Elworthy) within the boundary of the former Royal Forest. Nor were the Normans hungry for the wasteland. Only three undoubted Norman fortifications can be traced within the Exmoor National Park: Bury Castle, near Dulverton, Holwell Castle in Parracombe and Dunster Castle which, despite its added splendours, began like the others as an ordinary motte-and-bailey.

The highest point on Exmoor is Dunkery Beacon which stands
1,704ft above sea-level and is particularly familiar to readers of
Lorna Doone. The ancient hearths on its summit are survivals from
the time when the hill was indeed used as a beacon to warn of the
approach of an enemy

The reader will by now be aware of an apparent contradiction: the historical summary just given has emphasised the emptiness of Exmoor, yet the introductory paragraphs of this chapter stressed the intermingling of farmscape and wildscape, suggesting that settlement is now widespread. In the words of the now-defunct National Parks Commission (Thirteenth Report), the present-day Exmoor scene is best characterised by the word 'intimate'. How, then, did isolation and emptiness reign for so long? What dramatic changes in land use account for the transformation? The answers are found in twin historical events of the greatest importance: Exmoor remained a Royal Forest until 1819 and in that same year John Knight began the immense work of reclamation that created the Exmoor that we know today.

The misty origins of the Royal Forests of England are beyond the scope of this chapter. It is sufficient to record that by the reign of Henry II Exmoor was 'a definite tract of land within which a particular body of law was enforced, having for its object the preservation of certain animals *ferae naturae*'. The law was Forest Law, and the animals were the wild red deer.

Exmoor, in other words, was royal property. Under the provisions of Forest Law it was ruled over by its Warden who was answerable not to Common Law but to the king. The boundaries of the Forest shifted many times in 750 years. In some periods the Forest occupied all the territory now comprising the National Park. At other times 'the frequent cries of the oppressed' brought about a contraction of the Forest. For many years before it was sold to John Knight its boundaries corresponded to those of the 20,000 acres still referred to as 'The Forest'.

Yet, large or small, it was the dominant factor in Exmoor's life. Royal ownership prevented the sale of land. The preservation of the deer and the operation of Forest Law arrested agricultural development both within the Forest and on its fringes. True, the commoners of Hawkridge and Withypool received valuable concessions, but these were in return for burdensome duties.

Defoe's famous description of Exmoor as 'a filthy barren waste' was not even a half-truth. The moorland was, in fact, a vast summer grazing ground for sheep, cattle and ponies, the revenue from which was sufficiently ample to make the Wardenship a lucrative office. It was in return for acting as 'tellers' and 'drifters' that the commoners received their rights. Every head of sheep and cattle was counted on and off the Forest. Every grazing due was entered in the Forest Book; every unlawful beast was impounded.

But, clearly, the full potential of the moorland could not be realised under such a static system. John Knight's dream when he bought the Forest (and much land outside its boundaries) was to transform his backward kingdom into an up-to-date and well managed agricultural estate. His work and that of his son, Sir

Frederic Knight, created the Exmoor that we know today. Between them they established the guide lines along which sound Exmoor farming must proceed.

Failures they both knew. John Knight attempted orthodox four-course crop rotation and corn growing. Frederic tried to exploit the iron deposits in the Barle valley. Yet their failures were insignificant when compared with their successes. They made the present roads. They created every farm that now exists within the Forest boundaries. They broke land from the moor with ox teams and steam ploughs. They limed the sour land, and not a field they made has ever reverted. They imported the right stock. They discovered the root, rape and kale cropping that enables the breeding flocks to be wintered and supports the sheep-ranching that is Exmoor's best agricultural policy. This policy at once exploits the moor's natural resources and best guarantees access and unimpaired amenity.

In a word, they colonised Exmoor. The former royal demesne land—an extra-parochial wilderness—became an ecclesiastical and civil parish. Simonsbath is their creation. Their little moorland 'capital' became the centre of a thriving community. The dead hand of the Forest lifted its heavy weight. The moor came alive, and all the settlements in the purlieus were invigorated.

Few visitors to the Exmoor National Park realise that its landscape—that very beauty for which they seek it out—is largely man-made. Its cultivated farmland they recognise as 'tamed' or 'domesticated'; but fail to understand that the open moors are hill farms, their vegetation controlled by grazing and by 'swaling' (burning) that is a necessary part of moorland maintenance. Less than one-third of the total area of the park falls into the open moorland category and almost all of that—privately owned and, therefore, necessarily affected by the need to be profitable—is susceptible to changes in farm management that can produce quite quickly dramatic impacts on landscape.

As has been shown, the great Knight reclamation established a sound farming that survived almost unchanged until after World War II. It was a type of hill farming, modified to Exmoor's needs and peculiarly well suited to preserve moorland beauty while ensuring modest profits. Above all, it was a farming system that first established and then preserved the Exmoor way of life. Access to open moorland was never a problem. The huge moorland sheep walks had few enclosures; Exmoor farmers were traditionally hospitable to the comparatively few walkers who came their way in pre-park days.

Since World War II, and with increasing momentum since the designation of the park in 1954, hill farming on Exmoor has been modified by subsidy pressures and the impact of the annual agricultural price reviews. Forestry and agriculture inevitably responded to these influences, with the result that much open moorland was enclosed. There is little point in re-activating the controversies of the late sixties when a sharp debate about the precise extent of annual moorland loss temporarily embittered Exmoor life. The careful researches of the Exmoor Society, the steady pressure of the park authorities and the growing co-operation of the National Farmers Union and Country Landowners' Association have brought about a much healthier situation, culminating in the adoption of a policy designed to maintain the appearance and use of 'critical amenity areas'.

It is worth remarking at this point that full and effective implementation of that policy depends not upon the energy and determination of the park authorities but upon legislation to amend the Countryside Act of 1968. Sections 11 and 14 of that Act were presumably intended to provide powers to prevent the change of moorland character. Yet experience has shown that,

in this respect, the Act is more remarkable for its pious intentions than for its effectiveness. The blunt and uncomfortable fact remains that neither the Ministry of Agriculture nor the Department of the Environment has yet shown any sign of facing Exmoor's problem. The simple and traditional type of moorland farming no longer provides adequate returns: the grant-aided agricultural operations (draining, fertilising and ploughing) change the moorland scene. Some way must be found of paying the Exmoor farmer to remain a hill farmer.

Yet there is general agreement that the biggest threat to the park is external. Full understanding of the magnitude of the peril depends upon a knowledge of Exmoor's fragmented landscape. A grid pattern of roads divides the whole area into small parcels of countryside which vary in character from open and 'unimproved' moor (heather or grass) to wooded valleys and upland stock farms. Only the high plateau of The Chains and the 'middle moor' (Badgworthy to Alderman's Barrow) provide *extensive* stretches of uninterrupted wildscape. It is generally accepted that the two east-west routes (the A39 and the B3224/8) will have to be widened to cope with the increased traffic of the future. But major 'improvements' to the north-south routes or to the superb and lonely southern ridgeway would destroy the moorland's peace and solitude by channelling cars and coaches through the critical amenity areas. Similarly, Dulverton and Dunster, already under extreme pressure in the season, require relief roads; but the planning and routing is a delicate operation. The roads must be made to fit the landscape and to take the weight off these hard-pressed settlements. They

Lynmouth in North Devon is a fishing village within Exmoor National Park, which takes in the Bristol Channel coast from Combe Martin to Minehead. Many of the houses in the park are still thatched and retain their traditional characteristics

Much of Exmoor is intensively farmed and the importance of obeying the country code in such an area is paramount. Even here, in an apparently wild stretch of Doone Valley, a gate carelessly left open can cause much annoyance to farmers

must not be 'speedways' capable of rushing cars through to the next moorland bottleneck.

The traffic projections are frightening. The Bristol to Exeter motorway—necessary though it is—will be Exmoor's greatest enemy. In 1972 nearly 5 million people lived within $3\frac{1}{2}$ hours' driving time from the park: by 1981 that figure may have risen to 19 million. Large car parks at the entrance points and minibus services to selected 'honeypots' within the park will eventually be essential if Exmoor is not to be choked

to death by car-borne visitors.

Because of its intimate landscape and limited wildscape, Exmoor is extremely vulnerable. Continuing depopulation, decreasing employment and increasing dependence on 'the season' add to its problems. The chief recreational pleasures that it can offer to its visitors—riding, walking, fishing, wildlife—are incompatible with an uncontrolled increase in the numbers of visitors and are wholly dependent upon the maintenance of a stable and reasonably prosperous native population. Empty villages and roofless farmsteads would signal the cessation of that continuous and indigenous man-management of the park upon which its amenity value rests.

The serious explorer of Exmoor must proceed in a methodical way if he is ever to make head or tail of its bewildering topography. Seven basic routes may be discerned, each opening up characteristic and yet dramatically contrasting scenes. These routes are: the southern ridge; the Barle valley; the Exe valley; The Chains; the Badgworthy moorland or 'middle moor'; the Exmoor coast; Dunkery and the Brendons. There can be no dogmatism about favourite spots, finest combes or loveliest hills. Judgement is inevitably subjective. Yet, if I were to attempt a selection of Exmoor walks that would give the newcomer the feel of this elusive park, the choice would have to be something like this.

Warren Farm (in Exe Cleave) on a still October evening. The grey, Knight-built farmhouse dreams in the slanting sun; its shelter belt of trees casts long shadows; the green of its inbye fields shines against the yellowing *molinia* of the surrounding moor. Two foxes are basking on a grassy mound perched above the infant river. On the western skyline, where the moorland contours roll, a Forest stag appears: a lordly fourteen-pointer, making for the Exe and the farmland where he finds his evening meal.

Or out by the Longstone on an April day. The sweet bubbling call of the curlew. Cotton grass nodding. The ground squelching. Chapman Barrows swelling in the distance. A sudden squall of cold rain brings back memories of the winter wind that whirls the flying bent and takes the breath from your lungs. Then the sun again, with its promise of summer and 'worts'.

Alderman's Barrow on a winter day. The meet—most characteristic of Exmoor scenes—is over. I am on my way to Black Barrow where I always see the ponies. Across wet, tussocky ground; heading into the wind; the rain stinging. I must be mad to do it, but I'm making for Badgworthy and 'Doone Country', then downstream to Malmsmead where I have friends who, now the season is over, will have time to talk.

Christmas Day on Winsford Hill. No cars, no picnickers, no radios now. Snow coming in over the coast, horizontal on a northern gale. The ponies gather; thrust their rumps into the shelter of a beech hedge; patiently await the long winter. It is time to go. Only the deer and the ponies are safe 'up over' when the snow comes or darkness falls.

Exmoor—fierce, gentle, wild, tame, fragile. Infinite in mood and scene. Home to a handful: pleasure land of thousands. At risk.

Chapter 3

BRECON BEACONS

Margaret Davies

AREA: *519 square miles (134,400ha)*

ALTITUDE: *200–2,907ft (61–886m)*
        Pen y Fan 2,907ft (886m)
        Corn Du 2,863ft (872m)
        Waun Fach 2,660ft (810m)
        Brecknock Fan 2,632ft (802m)

ADMINISTRATION: *The Brecon Beacons National Park Committee has 27 members. 18 are appointed jointly by the County Councils of Powys (8 representatives), Gwent (2), Dyfed (2) and Mid-Glamorgan (2), including 4 nominated by the District Councils. 9 members are appointed by the Secretary of State for Wales.*

POPULATION: *38,600. Brecon, 6,304; Crickhowell, 1,287.*

COMMUNICATIONS: *There are rail services to Abergavenny on the eastern, and to Llandeilo, Llangadog and Llandovery on the western margins of the park. Infrequent buses run from Cardiff to Brecon via Merthyr Tydfil, and from Abergavenny to Brecon along the A40.*

By road Abergavenny to Brecon is 20 miles; Llandovery – Brecon 21 miles; Cardiff – Brecon 42 miles.

VIEWPOINTS *with or near car parks:*
Black Mountain (SN 732192)
Blaen Onneu (SO 157166)
Llangorse Common (SO 128273)
Storey Arms (SN 982203)
Sugar Loaf (SO 270182)
Torpantau (SO 049168)

NATIONAL PARK INFORMATION CENTRES:
Abergavenny. Lower Monk Street; tel Abergavenny 3254 (SO 299143)
Brecon. 6 Glamorgan Street; tel Brecon 2763 (SO 045285)
near Libanus, Brecon. Brecon Beacons Mountain Centre; tel Brecon 3366 (SN 977262)
Llandovery. 8 Broad Street; tel Llandovery 20693 (SN 767343)

OTHER VISITOR CENTRES, MUSEUMS:
Brecon. Brecknock Museum, Old County Hall (SO 045285)
Dan yr Ogof. Cave system (SN 840160)

NATIONAL PARK INFORMATION OFFICER, *Glamorgan Street, Brecon LD3 7DW*

Two centuries ago most of the South Wales coalfield was still beautiful pastoral countryside. Iron and coal working increasingly attracted people to it from the Brecon Beacons and much of the rest of upland Wales. Today many return frequently for leisure and refreshment in unspoilt landscapes over which sheep and cattle continue to graze. The colourful Brecon Beacons Park, where majestic Devonian scarps glow richly russet-red or brown, or glower crimson and black in storm and shadow, contrasts sharply with the grey-blue rocks of central Wales and with the mole-grey coalfield which lies immediately south of it. The park was intended for the people of the coalfield and of the line of former ironworking towns which runs from Ammanford to Brynmawr just beyond its southern boundary. Today it also has many day visitors from the West Midlands and the Bristol area.

Half-a-dozen south–north roads cross the park and provide a sample of its character. One is the Merthyr Tydfil-Brecon road (the A470). At the park boundary, two miles north-west of Merthyr, where limestone crags tower above a green valley, a scarred landscape destructively exploited to win iron and coal suddenly returns to its former beauty. On the limestone cliffs yews and rare whitebeams grow. Where other roads cross the limestones and sandstones of the south of the park the rivers tumble through gorges or disappear into caves and sink holes. There visitors can scramble along the gorges, notably along the headstreams of the river Neath.

On the A470 the road soon leaves the limestone and climbs gently into the red-brown rocks which cover most of the park. Soft water drains off the Devonian rocks and their spongy blanket of peat, and the motorist now passes, in the upper Taff valley, three reservoirs which have supplied Cardiff for eighty years. Former walled pastures around them carry conifer plantations while behind these, vast commons, well grazed by sheep and ponies, roll gradually up to the crests of the Brecon Beacons. As the motorist nears Storey Arms, at 1,440ft, snow screens flank the road. Used in turn by drovers, water engineers, youth hostellers and school field parties, Storey Arms is a starting point for paths up to Pen y Fan (2,907ft), a halfway house for ridgewalks along the crest of the Beacons and Fforest Fawr, a parking place for family parties and, in severe winters, for skiers and spectators.

From Storey Arms the road runs down Glyn Tarrell to Brecon. On either side the mountains rise up like petrified waves. Their cliffs turn their backs to the sun, and ice and snow linger on them in winter. In the Ice Ages these cliffs and cwms were filled with ice which ground into their slopes and gouged out their bottoms, often leaving small lakes there. One such cwm is Craig Cerrig Gleisiad on the left of the road, where arctic-alpine plants can be seen. As the road leaves the mountains and their apron of lower hills for the lush Usk valley, where well tended hedges replace stone walls, Brecon comes into view. Beyond it is the bastion of the Black Mountains, a great unbroken scarp which dominates the north-east of the park.

It takes not much more than an hour to drive to Brecon across the park from much of south-east Wales. Many are tempted to halt and explore en route. Brecon and other lowland settlements are beautifully set; often they have churches and castle mounds which are worth a visit. The Usk valley and the canal which follows it from Brecon to Abergavenny are lovely throughout the year; their autumn colours last long and dazzle and delight visitors. And as winter replaces autumn the high crests stand out clearly, dominating and sheltering the valleys.

From the Brecon Beacons, as from the Peak District, visitors from nearby conurbations return refreshed by walks in thin clean air over windswept mountains, pleasant strolls in limestone gorges or in the well tended countryside of the main river valleys.

Although the park lies in four different counties, landscape, geology, vegetation and land use make it a readily identified unit. It is dominated by four unique and tilted masses of red sandstone and brownstone which form some of the most noble and attractive plateaux of mountainous Wales. These Devonian rocks form, from west to east, the Black Mountain (Mynydd Du) of Dyfed; Fforest Fawr, the Great Forest of Brecknock; the Brecon Beacons proper and the

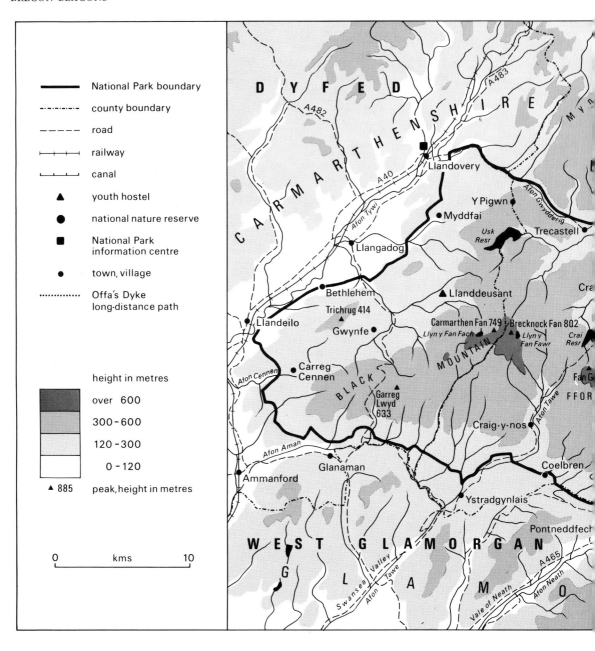

Black Mountains of Brecknock and Gwent. The first three rear up in steep scarps, deeply dissected by water and ice, to dominate the Usk valley and that of the Gwydderig, a tributary of the Towy. The eastern Black Mountains rise in a grand, less broken front from the valley of the Wye and its Llynfi tributary which flows through Llangorse Lake. All these magnificent mountains are deeply cut by beautiful valleys and all have long southern slopes covered by moorland and roll back gradually from the dominating cliffed scarps.

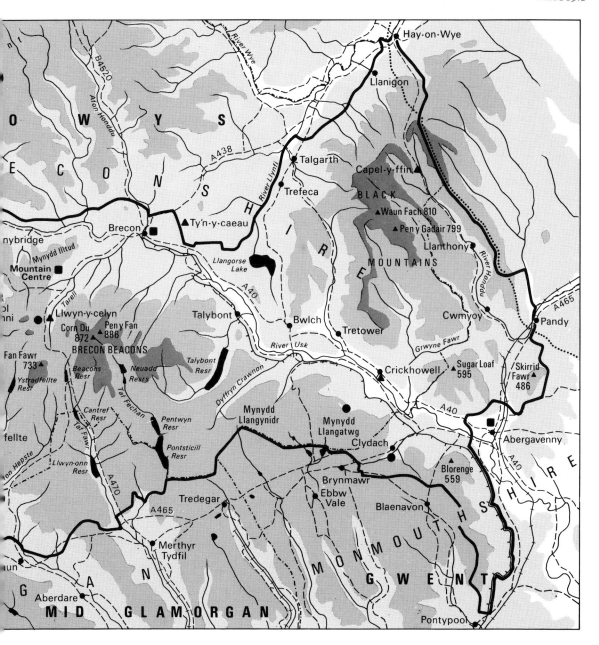

The culminating points of the Devonian scarps include the Carmarthen Fan (2,460ft) and Brecknock Fan (2,632ft) in Mynydd Du; Fan Gihirych (2,381ft) and Fan Fawr (2,409ft) in Fforest Fawr; Pen y Fan (2,907ft) and Corn Du (2,863ft) in the Brecon Beacons and Waun Fach (2,660ft) and Pen y Gadair (2,624ft) in the Black Mountains of Brecknock. Layer upon layer of interbedded sandstones and brownstones are exposed in their sometimes perpendicular scarps. The flat mountain tops are composed of resistant conglomerates and sandstones known

45

as Plateau Beds. Hard beds of conglomerates and sandstones also break the smooth fall of scarps and valley sides, standing out as cliffs or *tarenni*, locally known as *darrens*. An apron of lower hills with an underlying bed of softer red marlstones exists below the high scarps. In these contrasting lower hills between the peaks and the major valleys visitors will find interesting hamlets such as Llanigon and Llaneleu, quiet beauty and splendid views.

The Devonian rocks are not the oldest rocks of the park. Exposures of Ordovician and Silurian rocks cover most of mid-Wales and their eastern fringe reaches the surface on the slopes of the Towy valley between Llandeilo and Llandovery. These tough grits, shales and sandstones form the well wooded hillsides south of Llandovery and the ridge of Trichrug (1,360ft), and continue eastwards under the more recent rocks of Mynydd Du.

Throughout the southern fringe of the park the Devonian rocks themselves dip under the Carboniferous Limestone, Millstone Grit and Coal Measures which form the northern rim of the South Wales Coalfield. The heavily faulted limestones and coarse grits give rise to some of the most fascinating landscapes of the park. Deep wooded gorges in which rivers plunge over falls caused by hard rock bands, limestone surfaces pitted with sinkholes, long cave systems and craggy ridges are characteristic. Extensive clay-covered moorlands underlain by Millstone Grit in the south-west of the park are difficult to farm and abandoned holdings there have been largely planted with conifers in the past twenty years. But the grit outcrops of Mynydd Du are still used as common grazings and there the tough quartzites and conglomerates in the lowest layers of Millstone Grit form a ridge which rises to 2,080ft in Garreg Lwyd and produces the high hills between the Towy and Aman valleys.

The shales and sandstones of the Lower Coal

Series are best seen on the park's south-west border in the Aman valley, in the upper Tawe valley and on its south-east fringe near Brynmawr. A coal seam shows through the veil of water at Henryd Fall, a National Trust property near Coelbren, and both coal and iron outcrop in the Clydach gorge between Brynmawr and Abergavenny. The Coal Measures are the youngest and most readily eroded rocks of the park. Spoil heaps from early workings are largely grassed over; some even have a tree cover. Coal and ironstone seams along the north rim of the South Wales Coalfield dip gently and were readily worked by both primitive and post-war opencast methods, but there has been relatively little exploitation within what is now the park.

Landscapes underlain by carboniferous rocks show more disturbance by earth movements than the gently tilted Old Red Sandstone mountains which occupy most of the park. A major fault line can be walked south-west to north-east from the Vale of Neath at Pontneddfechan, through side valleys of the Taf Fawr and Taf Fechan, along the deep trough of Dyffryn Crawnon and across the Usk into the section of the Grwyne Fawr valley which lies between the Black Mountains and the isolated peak of the Sugar Loaf. On the line of this disturbance near Pontneddfechan, Craig y Dinas and Bwa Maen (stone bow) show obvious signs of folding and fracturing. Evidence of more recent and much smaller earth movements can be seen in the cleft slope of Skirrid Fawr, and in the leaning church tower of Cwmyoy, respectively three and six miles north of Abergavenny.

During the Ice Ages glaciers crept down the valleys from ice sheets on the park's summits, scraping some rocks bare by their grating action and masking others with gravel, boulders and clay from their moraines. Cwms which get least sun, such as those below northerly facing scarps, had their faces plucked away by ice and

Although much widened and altered by succeeding generations,
this bridge over the River Usk at Brecon has carried traffic for
over four centuries

retained it longest. Today they contain, in hollows between their cliffs and moraines, corrie lakes such as Llyn y Fan Fach and Llyn Fawr in Mynydd Du, and Llyn Cwm-llwch which lies below Pen y Fan. These lakes lie at heights of 1,600 – 2,000ft; beautiful and mysterious, they are the scenes of well known folk tales. The surface of Llangorse Lake, between outlying ridges of the Black Mountains, lies at only 502ft; it too is dammed behind a barrier of glacial gravel. Glacial clays and gravel were thickly spread on most hill and valley surfaces in the park and in the post-glacial millennia peat has developed as an uppermost layer, especially on the plateau tops and on the hillsides which slope gently towards the east and south borders of the park.

The main river of the Brecon Beacons National Park is the Usk. Major tributary valleys run towards it from all the park's mountains. Between Talgarth and Brecon the relatively low basin of the Llynfi forms the Talgarth Gap between the Usk and Wye valleys. The lowland pattern of rich green meadows, well kept hedges and woodlands is in splendid contrast with the open moorlands which sweep up from them.

This park is part of the upland core of Wales, and while it often bares its face to the sun to delight summer visitors, its mountains lie across the path of the prevailing south-west winds and attract a copious rainfall. At heights around 2,000ft on windward slopes the annual average rainfall is about 90in; in the Usk valley the average is about 40in. Higher totals fall on mountains like Pen y Fan while the Talgarth and Abergavenny neighbourhoods have less rain than other parts of the park. Snow rarely lies long except in northward facing cwms and on the highest ridges of the Black Mountains of Brecknock. In hard winters hillsides at Storey Arms, below Pen y Fan on the A470, may provide ski runs for several weekends.

High temperatures are unusual on the park's mountains. At 1,080ft at Cantref Reservoir, in the upper Taff valley, the range averages from $35 \cdot 7°F$ ($2°C$) in February to $57 \cdot 2°F$ ($14°C$) in August. The annual average of 1,368 hours of bright sunshine recorded at Cantref compares favourably with totals for the London area. In winter the hills often have clear skies when valleys in and around the park are filled with fog.

There are three national nature reserves and a variety of sites of botanical and geological interest in the Brecon Beacons Park. The nature reserves lie west of Abergavenny, in Cwm Clydach, where native beechwoods are found near their western limit of regeneration. At Craig y Ciliau, south of Crickhowell, massive limestone cliffs support rare *Sorbus* species and enclose the long cave system of Agen Allwedd, while at Craig Cerrig Gleisiad, six miles southwest of Brecon, there is a north-facing scarp with arctic-alpine plants like *Saxifraga oppositifolia*. There is also an ashwood at Penmoelallt, which is a forest nature reserve near the point where the A470 enters the park north-west of

Merthyr Tydfil. Here seedlings of *Sorbus leyana* are being raised; this and other whitebeams are not known outside the park.

The headstreams of the Neath run through gorges whose ashwoods are as interesting as the rocks on which they grow. Higher up are the enclosed pastures and vast commons where matgrass (*Nardus stricta*) is dominant. Purplegrass (*Molinia caerulea*), sphagnum and cottongrass give colour to wetter parts of the moorlands; the best heather moors are in the Black Mountains.

The great biological interest of Llangorse Lake is being gradually reduced by overenrichment of its waters and disturbance of its birds by power boats. But the great crested grebe and other fish-eating birds still breed there, it has a rich marsh flora, and white and yellow waterlilies, the fringed waterlily (*Nymphoides peltatai*) and the related buckbeam flower in the lake. The pike and eels of Llangorse Lake can reach a great size. Roach and perch breed there, as they do in the Wye and Usk, but these rivers are best known for their salmon and trout.

Visitors will find badger setts in many of the park's woods and may also see polecats; the species, like the buzzard, seems to be increasing in central Wales. In a park which has broad valleys that are lower than 200ft and mountains which reach almost 3,000ft there is a great variety of plant and animal life to absorb anyone who treads quietly in its countryside.

Since about 3000 BC man and his grazing animals have gradually modified nearly all landscape features in the Brecon Beacons Park. Only inaccessible precipices remain in their natural state; even the highest ridgetops have been crowned by cairns made by Bronze Age man and his successors. Mesolithic men hunted in the post-glacial forests around the park but no weapons have yet been found. Neolithic farmers, venturing up the Usk valley from the Severn estuary and the Cotswolds, made cultivation patches by cutting and burning the sparser stands of timber on gravel-strewn hillsides which slope down to the Usk and to the Talgarth Gap. Their family burials were in the stone chambers of long cairns which are similar to those of the Cotswolds; nine lie within the park. Their more humble houses have not been found. Neolithic burial chambers, now denuded of their cairns, lie by the A40 at Gwernvale, near Crickhowell, and at Tŷ Illtud, Llanhamlach.

Centuries of shifting cultivation by Neolithic farmers, and of browsing by their herds and those of the Beaker folk, would eat into the forests of the eastern half of the park. The Beaker folk and later Bronze Age people (1500-600 BC) buried their dead in stone-lined cists over which they raised round cairns. All were pastoralists and they appear to have spread into the south of the park from several points. Cairn burials suggest that, over the centuries, they mainly frequented Mynydd Du and the limestone country between the Taf Fawr and Neath valleys. Today these are exposed and treeless plateaux; they would have had a warmer climate in the Bronze Age and the farmsteads and small fields could in any case have been on hillsides below the hilltop tombs and open grazing land. In the upper reaches of the Tawe and Usk rivers, between the two main areas occupied in the Bronze Age, are three circles of standing stones which were probably used for ceremonial gatherings, as such circles were elsewhere in the early Bronze Age.

The use of iron for both weapons and farm implements spread into the area about 500 BC in a period which was wetter and stormier than the Bronze Age. Groups of Iron Age farmers lived and farmed in and around hilltop and hillside forts. The higher hills were deserted in favour of the slopes of the main valleys whose woods were felled to clear farmland and to build houses and stockades. The Towy, Usk and Llynfi rivers are all overlooked by Iron Age forts varying from those with single ramparts and ditches, like that above Crickhowell, to Pen-y-crug above Brecon where the defenders sheltered behind five ramparts. The great fort of Carn Goch, on a bracken-covered hill spur south of Bethlehem in the Towy valley, encloses 30 acres. Such forts would be built by sizeable groups. They banded together as the people known as the Silures who slowed down the Roman conquest of South Wales about AD 50.

The Roman forts and roads of the park are part of a network built to contain and control the Celtic hill folk. The main Roman fort was Y Gaer (ie The Fort), west of Brecon, and roads probably radiated from it along the Usk and Wye valleys and southwards across Fforest Fawr to Coelbren fort. One Roman villa has been found in the Usk valley at Llanfrynach and another above the River Towy near Llangadog, but most Romano-British farmers preferred the security of the English lowlands and the native farmers are unlikely to have had many competitors for their land. These Celtic farmers imprinted a pattern of small villages surrounded by ploughed fields and, beyond them, open grazing lands which was characteristic of the better land of the park until the eleventh century when the Norman conquerors took over the main valleys and feudalised their Welsh communities.

The Normans' route led them into the Welsh princedom of Brycheiniog, along the Wye valley and through the Talgarth Gap to Brecon. From Brecon they subdued the Usk valley and the lowlands near it. On their invasion routes they erected mottes with wooden keeps and, later, motte and bailey castles with stone keeps. They can be seen at Crickhowell, Brecon and Trecastle, all on the A40. Its eastern fringes were controlled from Abergavenny; the control

The view from the church at Patrishow, a remote village in the Grwyne Valley of the Black Mountains, is just one of the many scenic panoramas within the National Park

centre for the Towy valley was Carmarthen. As the Norman hold strengthened, walled boroughs with strong castles developed, often with Benedictine priories in the shelter of the castle walls. None of the towns of the park has the 'chessboard' street plan of North Welsh towns planned by Edward I, but all have one or other characteristic Anglo-Norman feature and Brecon, headquarters of Bernard Neufmarché, conqueror and first Marcher Lord of Brecon, shows them best. The town retains parts of its walls and lies below the castle and the adjoining priory, now the cathedral.

Once safely installed in their castles, the Norman knights organised a manorial pattern of husbandry throughout the lowlands. Arable fields and meadows were worked by serfs and pastures were grazed in common. A similar pattern prevailed in the hills, the Welshries of Brecon Lordship, and in Welsh manors above the Towy valley. The latter area remains Welsh speaking today. In the Welshries small clusters of cottages lay near the Welsh lord's house but farmsteads were also scattered beyond the common fields. These dispersed hill farms, with their fields grouped around them and with access to the common grazing land above, gradually multiplied in both hills and valleys, particularly after the fourteenth century when enclosure of the common fields increased.

In the heart of the park, Fforest Fawr was set aside in medieval times as a royal hunting forest, the Great Forest of Brecknock. Its valleys were once more heavily wooded than they now are, but much of it is over 1,500ft high and its main use, until its enclosure in 1819, was as common pasture for the adjoining farms. The higher parts of the Brecon Beacons proper are also common land, and manorial rights there, together with farms in the Tarell valley which use the land to pasture sheep, have recently been bought by the National Trust. Its other holdings in the park include the striking peaks of Skirrid Fawr and the Sugar Loaf in Gwent.

The Tudor monarchs had many links with Wales; among Henry VII's forces at Bosworth were Carmarthenshire (now part of Dyfed) men led by Sir Rhys ap Thomas of Dynevor, near Llandeilo, and of the spectacular castle of Carreg Cennen in the south-west of the park. Welsh squires prospered and built fine houses; the Tudor descendants of David Gam built Newton on the west side of Brecon. The Vaughans enhanced their fortified manor house at Tretower which had been initiated in the fourteenth century. It adjoins the ruins of the square keep built by the Norman knight Picard and replaced later by a round keep. Sequences of fortified and domestic architecture can be readily seen in the countryside and small towns of the Brecon Beacons Park.

In the eighteenth century there were forges at Brecon and on streams in the south of the park; they often worked pig iron supplied by iron-works beyond its boundary. The swift streams also powered woollen mills. But farming was and is the mainstay of this rural area and its main contributions to the adjoining coalfield were its people, its farm produce, its woods (which were felled to make charcoal) and its limestone and silica which were used by the iron, and, later, steel industries. Depopulation, deforestation and quarrying have all left their marks on the landscape. Small well designed factories are being set up in Brecon and in towns like Abergavenny beyond the park border, but apart from farming, service industries provide most jobs in the park.

Urban areas south of the park need water and by the late nineteenth century most of their local supplies had been utilised. Large reservoirs began to be built around the Brecon Beacons and there are now sixteen in the park. Recently the beautiful Senni basin, the only major valley without one whose open moorlands are grazed by the flocks of a close-knit community, was reprieved from the building of yet another reservoir for Cardiff.

Many urban visitors to the park have no links with its people and little appreciation of the problems of this part of upland Wales. Signs of depopulation in the form of broken walls of farmsteads and fields are common and many abandoned holdings have been planted with conifers. The Forestry Commission has over 20,000 acres of plantations in the park; as they mature they will provide more jobs and timber for sawmills and pulpmills. There are some attractive groupings of species in the newer plantations and good picnic sites in the older-established ones.

In the past decade abandoned farmsteads and cottages have increasingly become second or retirement homes. Where they are isolated and are not needed by local young couples their use as second homes is more acceptable than dereliction.

The lowest land in the park lies around 250ft at Hay-on-Wye and around 200ft by the Usk near Abergavenny. Much of the remainder is

Pen y Fan at 2,907ft is the highest mountain in the Brecon Beacons
National Park and its steep scarps and flat summit are characteristic
of the region

between 1,000 and 2,500ft high with thin soils on steep slopes and difficult winter weather. Arable land is limited and is found mostly in the Usk valley and beyond it as far as Talgarth. Farms there also carry milk and beef herds, as they do in the land which overlooks the Towy. The hill farms often have access to common grazings; they concentrate on rearing livestock for fattening on lowland farms. Pony rearing for local trekking centres is increasing as are farm holidays. The wealth of rural Wales lies in its grass; quality has improved greatly on the lower mountain flanks and valleys of the park. Destruction of hedgerows is small in scale in this pastoral countryside and such heather moors

as have succumbed to the plough, again in relatively few areas, have been trench-ploughed prior to afforestation.

The Brecon Beacons lie nearer to much of south-east England, including most of the London area, and even Brighton, than any other national park. Completion of the English section of the M4 improved access from them to the park as did the Severn Bridge from the Bristol area. Day visits from the Midlands, particularly to the Black Mountains and Llangorse Lake, have increased since first the M50 and then the M5 were completed. The eastern half of the park is naturally under greatest pressure from visitors using motorways and the Severn Bridge; Mynydd Du and its fringes are still the preserve of walkers and local motorists. Six major roads run from south to north through the park and the A40 runs from Abergavenny to Llandovery across it. All these roads carry increasing commercial traffic.

Gwent, Glamorgan and the district of Carmarthen have counter attractions. There is the Wye Valley and Gower, both areas of outstanding natural beauty, the Vale of Glamorgan and its coast, and the upper Towy valley. Since the Countryside Act, 1968, was passed all have planned or set up country parks in their own counties as magnets for the gregarious motorists who might otherwise drive into the Brecon Beacons Park. But as car ownership increases the tide of motorised visitors continues to flood into the park on fine weekends throughout the year.

In the post-war years during which the 1949 Act was framed, petrol was rationed and pleasure motoring in the countryside was not the fashionable pursuit that it is today; summer evening drives into the park, commonplace now, were rare in 1949. The southern boundary was drawn close to the former iron and steel towns so that the moorlands which had not been despoiled by industry could remain as open country within walking distance of their people. Walkers in the higher hills came by bus and by railways like the Merthyr-Brecon line, now defunct, which were in themselves good scenic routes. These earlier users of the park had a keen appreciation and understanding of its landscape, as have many of today's hill walkers.

This situation continued well into the 1950s with car-borne visitors gradually increasing throughout. The 1960s have seen the private car dominant and a great increase in the use of the park for adventure training and field studies. The leaders' briefing of some school and military parties could be much more thorough than

at present for with nearly seventy centres of various types in the park, proper organisation is becoming more and more essential.

Annual visitor surveys by Monmouthshire wardens at selected points (such as car parks) during Bank Holiday weekends indicate how visitor use has increased. The totals for 1965 and 1970 are: parking: 3,095 and 11,400; walking: 648 and 3,554; pony trekking: 104 and 1,140; boating: 196 and 1,510; cycling: 67 and 196.

The majority of visitors to the park want to enjoy its scenery from within or near their cars and need car parks, scenic laybys, picnic places and lavatories. The park authorities realise that the twenty car parks built for them since 1960 are not enough. This has been a period of 'squeezes', and private bodies as well as national funds, have contributed to building amenities of every sort. Thousands of visitors drive to the Brecon Beacons Mountain Centre, five miles south-west of Brecon. Late in 1972 its visitor total reached a million. It was built with generous help from the Carnegie United Kingdom Trust, was opened in 1965 and is maintained by grants from the constituent counties and from the government. It is fitting that descendants of those who worked under other ironmasters are numerous among those who take refreshment there and enjoy its views. The building, very well designed by the late S. Colwyn Foulkes, sits well on the gentle south slope of Mynydd Illtud.

The Brecon Beacons Park needs, for the use of its own people as well as for visitors, a residential study centre in an area like that around Crickhowell which is full of geological and biological interest. Many sports can be better catered for outside the park and the swimming pool and other facilities at the new Abergavenny Comprehensive School will be open to the public. Provision of such facilities in a 'buffer zone' outside the park boundary could be part of its future management. Information centres for the park already exist outside it at the Abergavenny and Llandovery gateways to it. The Mountain Centre partly functions as an information centre and the centre in Brecon, together with the county's good museum nearby, should not be missed by discerning visitors. The park's information services are co-ordinated by an officer stationed in Brecon.

In 1972 both the Brecknock and Monmouth sections of the park had one head warden. Brecknock also had an assistant warden and 84 voluntary wardens; in the smaller Monmouth section 20 volunteers and, in the summer, five part-time wardens man the service. Dinefwr lacks a warden service. The wardens make contact with all users of the park and when more realistic government grants are available the number of full- and part-time wardens needs to be considerably increased. Maintenance squads could carry out the manual work which they now do. The multifarious tasks accomplished by the present dedicated wardens include functioning as roving information officers. This aspect of the work of these knowledgeable men could surely be shared and supplemented seasonally by part-time wardens who might be teachers available during holiday months. Such wardens could guide interested visitors, or provide self-guiding trails with diagrammatic plaques at many points in the park. The faulted rocks and falls in the gorges of streams which join to form the River Neath could be demonstrated in this way, as could the ecology of Llangorse Lake. Possibly we may one day see a warden in his launch telling the story of the Brecon and Monmouthshire Canal and its tramroads as he takes a party along it. This canal runs for 32 miles from Brecon to Pontypool, mainly along hillsides above the Usk. It was built to carry iron to Newport and tramroads linked it to the main ironworks. Commercial use ceased in 1932, but since 1968 the British Waterways Board has restored it for recrea-

tional use, with financial help from the Welsh Office and the counties through which it runs. Pleasure cruising and facilities for it are increasing, as are walking and fishing on its pleasant towpath.

The limestone cliffs which rise above the canal, near Crickhowell, contain Agen Allwedd (Key Fissure), one of the longest British cave systems, although recent surveys of Ogof Ffynnon Ddu (Black Spring Cave) show that it is even longer. The latter cave is in the upper Tawe valley and most caving in the park is concentrated in the Tawe basin and in that of the Neath and its headstreams. The land surfaces between them are pitted with sinkholes and cut by intermittent streams and many cave systems remain to be surveyed. Dan yr Ogof cave system in the Tawe valley is open to the public and the entrance to Porth yr Ogof near Ystradfellte can also be explored when the River Mellte is not in spate.

From 1974 the Brecon Beacons National Park will be administered by one park planning committee led by a national park officer of senior status. Realistic exchequer contributions to provide him with supporting staff are promised, and the team will prepare and implement a management plan for the park as a unit. Management and guidance of visitors, whether they be motorists or pedestrians enjoying a variety of open air activities, will need to be planned so that they do not hinder the day-to-day activities of the people of the park. Experience in the past twelve years suggests that, except on its eastern fringe, paths over farmland, particularly near settlements and popular roadside halts, are inadequately signposted and waymarked. A few Brecknock farmers have waymarked their own paths; more could co-operate in this way. The footpath network needs to be rationalised and parts of it need not be signposted. More unobtrusive information plaques are needed on site, as are more nature trails which might draw visitors away from the three national nature reserves and other ecologically important areas in the park. Land which is vital for national park but not for farming purposes might be taken into various types of public ownership. Gwent is thus acquiring part of the Blorenge mountain, which towers above Abergavenny, for parking, picnicking and sightseeing, and the National Trust has many holdings in the park.

Young farmers' clubs in the area have joined other groups in voluntary work in the park. They have helped to build picnic furniture for laybys and have invited young townsfolk to some lively conferences. In future years they may, if they wish, contribute considerably to the provision of grant-aided and well sited accommodation and picnic sites on their land and to the management of casual visitors to it.

In the United States, land in national parks is largely owned by the nation and its people take pride in them. British parks could be managed so that both inhabitants and visitors could be proud of them as vital parts of the national heritage. At present in Wales the media publicise criticism of national parks, much of it originating in rival farmers' unions, and ignore the devoted service given to them by officers and committee members who have worked with minimal government support. Visitor pressures bear heavily on most of rural Britain, but it is in the parks that special and increased funds and staff will be available for conservation and improvement so that visitors' enjoyment of them benefits both them and the people of the parks. The Brecon Beacons National Park is beautiful and largely unspoilt but its planning team will need to think carefully if the scars of unwise use are not to disfigure its landscape for future generations.

Chapter 4

PEMBROKESHIRE COAST

John Barrett

AREA: *225 square miles (58,350ha)*
ALTITUDE: *0 – 1,760ft (0 – 537m)*
Foel Cwmcerwyn 1,760ft (537m)
ADMINISTRATION: *The Pembrokeshire Coast National Park Committee, a separate committee of the Dyfed County Council, has 18 members of whom 12 are appointed by the County Council; 10 represent the County Council, and 1 each the District Councils of Preseli and South Pembrokeshire. 6 members are appointed by the Secretary of State for Wales.*
POPULATION: *21,800. Tenby, 4,985.*
COMMUNICATIONS: *There are rail services to Fishguard, to Haverfordwest and Milford Haven, all close to the park, and to a few stations in the park, including Tenby, on the line to Pembroke.*

Bus services survive on a number of routes in the park, with connections to national coach networks. During the summer holidays of 1973 and 1974 an experimental 22 seater midibus service sponsored by the national park authority has operated on the coast road from Newgale to Dale.
VIEWPOINTS *with car parking:*
Bwlchgwynt (SN 073321)
Fishguard Bay (SM 962375)
Minwear Woods (SM 059141)
Newgale Sands (SM 854208)

The Ridgeway (SS 090999)
Wooltack Point (SM 761089)
NATIONAL PARK INFORMATION CENTRES:
Broadhaven. Pembrokeshire Countryside Unit, The Car Park; tel Broadhaven 412 (SM 864140)
Fishguard. The Town Hall; tel Fishguard 3484 (SM 958370)
Haverfordwest. Pembrokeshire County Museum, The Castle; tel Haverfordwest 3708 (SM 953157)
Kilgetty. Kingsmoor inf centre; tel Saundersfoot 3672 (SN 121071)
Milford Haven. The Town Hall; tel Milford Haven 2501 (SM 908058)
Pembroke. Drill Hall, Main Street; tel Pembroke 2148 (SM 985015)
St David's. The City Hall; tel St David's 392 (SM 753253)
Tenby. The Norton; tel Tenby 2402 (SN 132008)
OTHER VISITOR CENTRES, MUSEUMS:
Haverfordwest. Pembrokeshire County Museum, The Castle (SM 953157)
Scolton. Scolton Manor Museum and Country Park (SM 990220)
Tenby. Tenby Museum, Castle Hill (SN 138005)
NATIONAL PARK INFORMATION OFFICER, *County Offices, Haverfordwest SA61 1QZ, Wales*

When the Pembrokeshire Coast National Park was designated in 1952 the 168 miles of cliffs, sandy bays, deeply indented valleys and the great harbour of Milford Haven were almost unmarked by the greedy hand of man. Included were the coastal Presely Hills, unchanged since the Iron Age, and further south the Daugleddau estuary, fringed by antique oakwoods where shelducks nest in safety. We seemed then to have made sure that the beauties of wild Atlantic coast, peaceful estuary and timeless hills would be passed on intact for future generations to enjoy.

For years the park committee was condemned as no more than an impediment to the making of easy money along the coast. No minister, nor the National Parks Commission (as it was), ever insisted that higher standards of design must be applied within the park than outside it. The statutory obligation 'to make available' has so dominated the obligation to preserve, that visitors to the Saundersfoot-Tenby-Penally sector now find unspoilt countryside only by leaving the designated area. The creeping blight of chalets and 'villas' will destroy St David's and Dinas and Newport within ten years unless a more determined and coherent public opinion stops it. Those who have struggled without adequate money, manpower or public support to maintain the beauty of Pembrokeshire's coast console themselves only by knowing how much worse things would have been without them. And much that is marvellous still survives. Ours is an antique land, wrapped round by the dragon-green and luminous sea. The sea dominates the land.

Round all the 168 miles of cliff runs a continuous long distance path. Even eighteen years after its designation four lengths had still to be established after the ceremonial opening in 1970. From the Carmarthen frontier at Amroth it passes Tenby, then follows the limestone cliffs of Lydstep and Stackpole Warren, skirting the Castlemartin tank range, and continues round the Angle peninsula. Here it doubles back up the Haven to the ferry between Pembroke Dock and Neyland, and turns westwards again round Dale, following the Atlantic coast, past Skomer, and around St Bride's Bay and St David's Head. Then it turns north-eastwards along tall and lonely cliffs by Trefin and Strumble, and passing

above Fishguard harbour, it climbs on through to Dinas Island, Newport, and Morfa, whence it follows a line to Cemais Head and the Cardigan boundary at St Dogmael's.

The rocks from which the Pembrokeshire landscape is hewn rise in a geological column from Pre-Cambrian times, some 3,000 million years ago, to the Coal Measures of 250 million years ago. Rocks deposited since then have all been eroded off again.

The Pre-Cambrian granites and volcanics appear round St David's, in the Roch-Treffgarne ridge and Goultrop cliffs. Cambrian rocks dominate the cliffs from Newgale to Whitesand; from Caerbwdi the purple sandstone was quarried for the cathedral. In the Ordovician shales which dominate the coast northwards from Trefin, are hard lavas and igneous blocks marking the skyline of Pencaer and Presely, Ramsey and Carn Llidi. Next upwards, beneath Silurian conglomerates, limestones and sandstones of the Marloes peninsula, is the Skomer Volcanic Series that stretches out to Grassholm and the Smalls.

At the end of Silurian times these lowest rocks were mightily disrupted by the Caledonian earth movements which imposed the SW-NE grain on the north of the county and produced the St David's peninsula.

Then red dust from a harsh desert consolidated in coastal lagoons. This Old Red Sandstone underlies the Dale peninsula, Milford Haven and some of the south coast. Three hundred and fifty million years ago, in a warm clear sea that deepened from the south, the Main Limestone accumulated, forming those grey cliffs from Linney to Stackpole, at Lydstep and Giltar Point. On top again, the Millstone Grit crops out at Druidston and Tenby, beneath the Coal Measures that accumulated as rising sea-level submerged the forests of 300 million years ago, and which now stretch from Saundersfoot

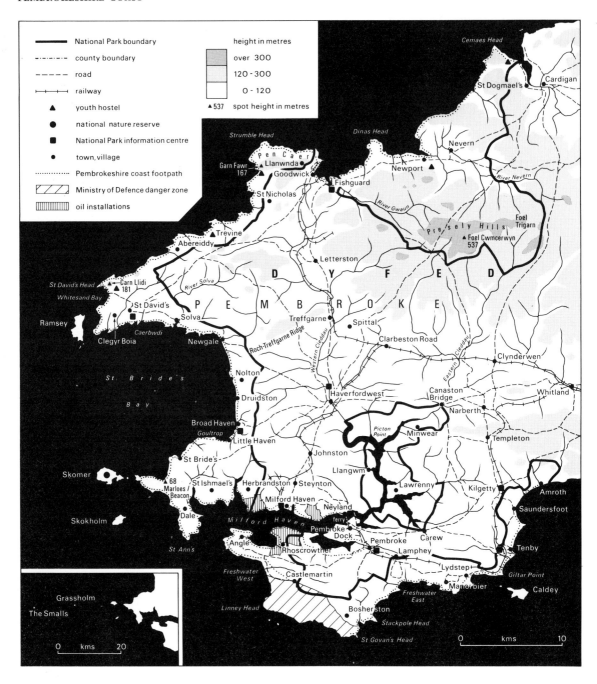

across the Cleddau to St Bride's Bay.

Next, the Armorican earth movements folded and faulted the Carboniferous and Old Red Sandstone and imposed the WNW-ESE grain upon them, while further contorting the more ancient systems in the north.

The flat surface that dominates the coastal scenery belies the geological complexities below.

It was cut by waves some 17 million years ago when sea-level was 200ft higher than now, with time to reduce all the sediments to sea-level but with not quite enough time to cut down the hard igneous intrusions which stand today as islands above the 200ft surface—Carn Llidi, Clegyr Boia, Garn Fawr, Marloes Beacon—just as our present stacks and islands stand above the present wave-cut platform.

As falling sea-level exposed this surface, streams and rivers began to impose the drainage pattern that is now so deeply incised. Valleys were further enlarged and the gorges of the Gwaun, Nevern, Alan and Solva were gouged out only 20,000 years ago by the erosive energy of meltwater from rotting ice as it roared down to a sea whose level rose to drown the lower courses of the rivers thus bringing warm Gulf Stream water into the heart of the county. Because of this frost is unusual along the coast and grass grows all the year.

The rainfall along the cliffs is 32in and this increases by an inch for every mile inland. Clouds clear fast enough to bring more sunshine along the coast than anywhere else on the mainland of Britain. The winds of heaven all blow, sometimes it seems at the same time, especially when the gales, with gusts of 100mph or more by no means exceptional, carry salt spray far onto the windward cliffs. For several miles inland trees survive only in deep valleys and the settlements of man need shelter just as much as water.

Before the last advance of the ice drove him south 50,000 years ago, Old Stone Age man left domestic refuse in caves on Caldy, at Hoyle's Mouth and Monkton. Ten thousand years ago, as the weather improved, men came northwards again. They are known almost only by the waste flakes that fell where craftsmen fashioned tools from flint near Solva, in Dale, at Frayneslake and on the Nab Head.

Then, 5,000 years ago, the first farmers arrived by boat, from the south, the stages of their journey being marked by the megalithic tombs they built for their dead—standing stones covered by a capstone that may weigh as much as 28 tons. The elegance of Pentre Ifan displays imaginative artistry. Consider Carreg Samson, Carreg Coitan Arthur, or Llech-yr-dribedd and New Stone Age men cease to be just savages in woad and wolfskin. Traces on Caldy and Clegyr Boia are almost all we have of daily life during the 2,000 years before the first man of the metal era passed by.

Bronze Age man came on foot from the east for copper from the Wicklow Hills. (How did he know it was there?) His tracks across Presely to Whitesand and along the Ridgeway to West Angle in the south are signposted by burial mounds. Stone circles at Dyffryn and Gors Fawr and many single standing stones add to the mystery of how these people lived. We have recently learnt that the Stonehenge bluestones were taken from Presely 500 years before Bronze Age men incorporated them in the inner circle. What sanctity was transferred in this laborious way? Why should a block of sandstone from the Cosheston Beds of the Old Red Sandstone occupy the Stonehenge focus now labelled the 'altar-stone'? The continuity and the multiplicity of strong echoes from former days hang in the Presely air. Does not Bedd Arthur mark Arthur's grave and there, in the sweeping bowl of Cwm Cerwyn, do not Cerrig Meibion Arthur stand in memory of the two sons killed by the boar Twrch Trwyth?

By about 300 BC the first men of the clanking age of iron came by sea, possibly from Brittany, and settled behind single defensive banks across narrow-necked coastal promontories. By 100 BC later-comers had developed complicated double-curving banks. Those who moved inland defended hilltops and steep bends in the sides of river valleys.

The Pembrokeshire long distance path runs along the whole of the
168 miles of the park's coast. Here, a bulldozer works on a stretch
near Dale

But who was it who built the great forts on Foel Trigarn and Garn Fawr and the 'regional capital' on Carn Ingli, massively defended by stone walls? Was this the indigenous Demetae or the Deisi moving across from Ireland in the first centuries AD, or were Celtic tribes being pushed westwards in those days? Pembrokeshire abounds in the evidence; it is the interpretation that is so largely lacking. The field system of St David's Head maintains a continuity of 2,000 years of agriculture. Hut-circles there, on Skomer and within the defended raths, taken with fragmentary excavated evidence, still paint only a hazy picture of how these people lived.

Surely the Christian message was first delivered in these Iron Age forts. The Fathers arrived by sea. From the first Christian days, saints were honoured by name along the coast. Prayers before the start and thanksgivings at the end of a stage were offered in chapels built hard by the tide and dedicated to men of example. Commanding the largest intersection of the busiest sea-routes in western Europe, inevitably a vigorous Christian community was centred in Pembrokeshire. By chance (or God's plan) David was the leader—David the water-drinker, David the puritan. The fame of the saint so resounded in Christendom that after his death all men hoped to visit his shrine. Then were the seaways busy with pilgrims and the sailors' chapels multiplied.

The years 400–800, the great Age of the

Saints, marks a prodigious contrast with the darkness elsewhere and reached out to standards and aspirations that exceeded anything achieved since then. The stones by which the holy men preached, which they used as symbols to illumine their good news, still bear witness to their undying faith.

The Vikings knocked down some of the Christian symbols when they dominated these western seas during the eighth and ninth centuries. Their language survives in coastal place-names; -*holmen*, a small, and *oy*, a large island, in Grassholm, Skokholm, Caldy and Ramsey; -*vik*, a safe anchorage, in Goodwick, and Musselwick; and Angle and Dale.

Despite the Norse blood in their veins the Normans came to Pembrokeshire by land and took for themselves the rich agricultural south which they defended by a line of castles, dominated by Pembroke, which stretched from Roch through Haverfordwest, Wiston, Llawhaden, Narberth and down to Tenby and Amroth. Behind these they imposed their manorial system manned by imported Irish and Flemish labour, leaving the old Welsh ways largely undisturbed in the north. This division into Welshry and Englishry survives in place-names, in committee arguments and the proportion of Welsh speakers in the villages. Even so, the divisions imposed by the Normans have been exaggerated. Their colonisation was more a process of absorption than expulsion. The evidence multiplies of the continuity of Welsh families owning land in the heart of Norman Pembrokeshire.

All round the coast rotting remnants of village quays, piers and warehouses survive from the days before the railways, when every coastal village was engaged in short- and long-distance trade often in coal or limestone, many in boats they built for themselves.

Some of these boats were literally the village shop. On 14 May 1831 a little schooner tied up at the Parrog at Newport and, in a twinkling, displayed for sale hops, prunes, ironmongery, vinegar, grocery, frying pans, soap, candles, chairs, hats, cider, tobacco, brandy, sweets, shot, guns, collars and ties. She was off again with the tide to set up shop at the nearest quay next day; in this way she worked her way back to Bristol where she took on fresh stocks. Haverfordwest was by far the busiest port and the pub on the quay is not named The Bristol Trader by accident. Some of the warehouses still survive and the mayor is still the Admiral.

The park is bewildering in its infinite variety —there are rocks of every acidity, at every angle, of every degree of hardness; there are some coasts fully exposed while others remain sheltered from the salt fury of Atlantic gales; there are estuaries, sand-dunes, and salt-marshes. There is intense peninsulation into the winter warmth of the North Atlantic Drift, and yet cold climate creatures are many; moorlands and mountain streams in rocky gorges co-exist with marshes overlying glacial clays, and bogs; it is a land as yet thinly populated, with small farms, small fields and many 'waste' patches, a land still mostly unpolluted by agricultural chemicals. A land of flowers.

On the cliffs they gather every year—the spring surge bringing celandines, scurvy grass and vernal squills, sea-pinks, ox-eye daisies and lady's-fingers. Great sweeps of bluebells appear, and the fragrance of primroses and hot gorse is the very air you breathe; stone-crop and spurrey are clothed in suits of orange and grey lichens studded with exquisite fruiting cups. In high summer the picture changes and forests of fox-gloves, wild carrot, cat's-ear and yellow tormentil sprinkle the bell-heather which, banked with thyme, contrasts with the deep tones of Welsh gorse. No catalogue can possibly convey this annual miracle of regeneration, augmented by soldier beetles, blue and copper butterflies,

61

Old cottages on the beach at Abereiddi huddle together beneath
the small tower on Trwyncastell, continually beaten by the sea

St Mark's flies, lizards and adders.

Along these cliffs choughs are increasing, so that now fifty pairs nest in caves and crannies; buzzards and ravens are common and peregrines again occupy three of their eyries. Fulmars are also multiplying, and stonechats flick their tails on bramble twigs.

The main lines of bird migration cross these western shores and from March to May and later in the autumn untold numbers pause for rest and food. Between Christmas and New Year the keen watcher will be able to recognise eighty-five species of birds and find forty kinds of plant in flower.

Something about the islands (which nobody really understands) draws large colonies of seabirds to nest there. More than 15,000 pairs of gannets on Grassholm are protected by the Royal Society for the Protection of Birds. On Skokholm and Skomer (and to a lesser extent on Ramsey where shipwrecked rats prey on birds' eggs), amongst all those flowers, puffins, razorbills, guillemots and many other species justify the designation of the islands as a national nature reserve. They are under the careful management of the West Wales Naturalists' Trust and the Royal Society for the Protection of Birds. But their life depends totally on the sea and so designation of an island reserve is meaningless unless the sea is clean.

The Atlantic grey seals who live all round the coast need clean water too. Even now their blubber contains 200ppm PCB, three times as much as anywhere else on the west coast of Britain, which must derive from poisonous food (PCB is a poison persisting in the sea from paint and plastic factory effluents). The seals congregate off Grassholm in summer and then disperse to mainland and island beaches, out of reach of the spring tides, to produce their pups in October.

Clean water is also necessary for the survival of the vast range of marine and shore creatures. The situation here is unlike anywhere else in Britain because the cold and warm water populations survive together, unchanged since Gosse rejoiced a hundred years ago in 'places that teem with treasures, where the naturalist may see, in a day's excursion, what in ordinary circumstances he would count a fair harvest in a week'.

Up the Cleddau estuary the oakwoods hanging on the river cliffs may be fragments of primeval vegetation. Unfortunately many were pollarded during World War I. A wildfowl refuge protects the ducks that winter there and at low tide clouds of waders feed on the mud across which rice-grass spreads. Greenshank winter in the hills where kingfishers dive for gobies. Salmon run in the river and, curiously, herring breed in the deep water off Llangwm.

Almost the whole park is owned by farmers, and the public has no right of access to it. Out of 3,466 holdings in the county, 1,558 are less than 50 acres and only 83 more than 300 acres. Smallness of size is usually accompanied by lack of capital, inadequate buildings, tiny fields and an increasing difficulty in maintaining an economic hold. Many smallholders are driven to catering for 'bed and breakfasts' to balance their budgets. All too often it is more profitable to grow caravans than corn.

Along the coast, arable farming is based on meat and milk. Some oats and barley are grown, largely for fodder. The almost frost-free climate allows potatoes to be planted early in March and to be lifted, in good years, in late May. Irrigation almost doubles the crop yields. Broccoli for harvesting at Christmas may follow the potatoes.

As rainfall increases inland, so does the emphasis on permanent grass and most farms produce meat and milk. Further inland still, cattle give way to sheep at about the 700ft contour. Improvements in upland pasture constantly increase the weight of meat per acre. On Presely ancient customs of common rights of sheepfarmers are protected by the Courts Leet of the Barony of Cemais.

Oil refineries straddle the park boundary; despite expensive earth movement and contour shaping, the visual impact is widespread and corrosive. The Milford Haven Conservancy Board (the harbour authority) has succeeded in keeping the Haven water clean. Careful monitoring reveals almost no biological changes and the techniques of cleaning up after an accident use only least harmful materials. All together the ramifications of the oil industry have generated something like 2,000 jobs.

The industry has grown bigger at a speed which is hard to credit. In 1956 only three tankers in the world carried over 30,000dwt, in 1961-5 405 others were built, and by 1966 half the world's construction was 150,000dwt or larger. In 1960 the Haven handled 2.8 million tons of oil traffic, in 1964 17.7 million, in 1966 28.9 million, and in 1970 41.2 million tons.

The channel of the Cleddau, drowned by post-glacial rising sea-level, is at least 50ft deep at all states of the tide. In 1958, simply because of this 50ft, the Esso refinery and BP ocean terminal were built. Since then Texaco and Gulf have added their piers and refineries and Amoco are building theirs now.

In 1967 the Board dredged to allow in 190,000

The Pembrokeshire Coast National Park abounds in beautiful and
as yet largely unspoiled coastal scenery. Here, at Whitesands Bay,
there seems little to disturb the serenity but further south around
Milford Haven industrial development makes way for oil

tonners, drawing 58ft, and then in 1968 another
£6 million was spent to accommodate 270,000
tonners, drawing 64ft, and these are already
using the Haven.

Only about 5 per cent of the refined products
leave by road and rail, the rest is re-exported in
what are laughably called 'coasting tankers'—
little boats of 30,000 to 50,000 tons. A jointly
owned pipeline to the Midlands and Mersey is
being built to carry 4 million tons a year. Three
companies pipe fuel to the CEGB power-
station which is outside the park but whose
700ft chimney intrudes aggressively. It also
pours out daily 650 tons of sulphur gases—gross

pollution preferred to including the full social
and biological cost in the price of the product.

The £10 million derived annually from the
tourist trade in Pembrokeshire is second in
importance only to agriculture. Many visitors
are refugees from the crowds in Cornwall and
Devonshire, saying that they seek simple peace
and quiet and release from the rat-race. Extra-
polation of curves suggests that to accommodate
the ever-increasing numbers something like
25,000 more beds must be provided in the next
five years (three times as much than at present in
Haverfordwest). If only proper standards of
design and, more important, siting could be

guaranteed, the £10 million could be £16 million without serious damage to the coastal splendour.

The Pembrokeshire Coast National Park Committee is confronted annually by 1,000 and more applications to develop in the park. The Committee aims to concentrate new building round existing nuclei; village plans delimit capacity; two small resorts, at Broadhaven and Freshwater East, will include larger facilities. All building at the edge of the Cleddau has been successfully resisted. The spread of static caravans has at last been halted, but until the Schedule of Exemptions is deleted from the Act, private organisations enjoy and proliferate a damaging privilege. Second homes multiply, each making some impact on the scene. Half the houses in some coastal villages are empty for most of the year.

Owners of land close to the sea have no predestined right to tourist-development income that is denied to owners somewhat further inland. If all the tourist accommodation was built two miles back from the coast (Haverfordwest is the obvious tourist centre), then the coast could be secured for future generations to enjoy as present visitors say they want to find it now. An equally firm restriction on private cars, coupled with abundant minibus services, is also necessary if every valley bottom is not to become a car park and the lanes leading to them destroyed by widening.

For lack of firm and farsighted political policy decisions to pass on intact the splendour we have inherited, the tourist industry continues to destroy the very base of its prosperity in Pembrokeshire.

The nightmare forecast in *The Economist* that the old-fashioned idea of a coastal park will be replaced by the largest petro-chemical complex in Europe may well prove true. The brochure issued by the Harbour Conservancy to enquiring industrialists indicates three positions for a deep-water pier off the Angle peninsula; that peninsula is wholly within the Pembrokeshire Coast National Park, is wholly unspoilt and would be wholly engulfed by the development of any one of these options. Yet no authority, local or national, has been prepared to insist on the deletion of these sites. Angle stands all the time on sacrificial offer to the false god GNP.

We know that measurements of waves and tides in St Bride's Bay have been expensively investigated; we know that refinery capacities are being increased, not always with a proportionate increase in pier capacity.

Further off-shore, exploration of the Celtic Sea may lead to vast increases in shore capacity and installations in Milford Haven. Once again, no minister and no authority is prepared to draw a map to define exactly where and how the landward end of these activities would and, more important, would not be acceptable. Only land held by the National Trust stands secure; for the rest, all past experience indicates that designation as national nature reserve, national park, heritage coast and the rest will count as nothing before the 'national interest' as defined by the tycoons.

The next five years are critical. Just when the park needs brave direction, the reorganisation of local government forces Pembrokeshire into Dyfed and imposes on the park a planning hierarchy and committee composition both distant and inexperienced. Without time available for settling down, events may overrun the new order.

Abba Eban believed that men will behave sensibly only when they have exhausted every other alternative; since we have just about run the whole gamut of foolishness there is still room for cautious optimism about the future of this lovely park.

Chapter 5

SNOWDONIA

William Condry

AREA: *840 square miles (217,559ha)*
ALTITUDE: *0 – 3,560ft (0 – 1,085m)*

> *Snowdon 3,560ft (1,085m)*
> *Carnedd Llywelyn 3,485ft (1,063m)*
> *Glyder Fawr 3,279ft (999m)*
> *Aran Fawddy 2,974ft (906m)*
> *Cadair Idris 2,927ft (892m)*

ADMINISTRATION: *The Snowdonia National Park Committee, a separate committee of the Gwynedd County Council, has 27 members. 18 are appointed by the County Council; 14 represent the County Council, 1 each the District Councils of Aberconway, Arfon, Dwyfor, and Meironnydd. 9 members are appointed by the Secretary of State for Wales.*

POPULATION: *26,900. Dolgellau, 2,564; Bala, 1,600.*

COMMUNICATIONS: *The North Wales coast line to Holyhead has stations convenient for the national park at Penmaenmawr, Llanfairfechan and Bangor. On the eastern edge of the park the line south from Llandudno Junction has several stations, including Llanrwst and Betws-y-coed, on its route to Blaenau Ffestiniog. In the south and west the Cambrian Coast line (from Shrewsbury or Aberystwyth to Pwllheli) goes via Dyfi Junction, Aberdyfi, Tywyn, Barmouth, Harlech and Porthmadog.*

The park has main roads encircling all the chief blocks of uplands. The towns and larger villages are mostly linked by bus services but some of these are infrequent.

Narrow-gauge railways, operating mainly in the summer, are: Llanberis to Snowdon summit; Llanberis Lake railway; Porthmadog up the Vale of Ffestiniog; Tywyn to Abergynolwyn (the Tal-y-

llyn line); Fairbourne to the Barmouth ferry; and Llanuwchllyn to Llangwair on the way to Bala.

VIEWPOINTS *with or near car parks:*
Aberglaslyn Pass (SH 598463)
Bala (SH 914357)
Barmouth Bridge (SH 625148)
Bwlch y Groes (SH 914230)
Nant Gwynant (SH 658543)
Soflen (SH 821567)

NATIONAL PARK INFORMATION CENTRES:
Aberdyfi. The Wharf; tel Aberdyfi 321 (SN 614959)
Bala. The Old British School, High Street; tel Bala 367 (SH 927361)
Blaenau Ffestiniog. Queen's Bridge; tel Blaenau Ffestiniog 360 (SH 698459)
Dolgellau. Bridge End; tel Dolgellau 422888 (SH 729179)
Harlech. Gwyddfor House, High Street; tel Harlech 658 (SH 581310)
Llanberis. Lakeside Drive; tel Llanberis 765 (SH 582599)
Llanrwst. Glan y Borth; tel Llanrwst 640604 (SH 799615)

OTHER VISITOR CENTRES AND MUSEUMS:
Blaenau Ffestiniog. Llechwedd Slate Caverns
Llanberis. Dinorwic Industrial Museum
Porthmadog. Railway Museum
Tywyn. Railway Museum

SNOWDONIA NATIONAL PARK RESIDENTIAL STUDY CENTRE: *Plas Tan-y-bwlch, Maentwrog, Blaenau Ffestiniog, Merioneth.*

NATIONAL PARK INFORMATION OFFICER, *Yr Hen Ysgol, Maentwrog, Blaenau Ffestiniog, Merioneth LL1 4HW*

Outlined black against a yellow evening sky Snowdonia's mountains make simple beautiful shapes. But next morning they are utterly different. Now the light is behind you and is getting into the mountain folds. You see that the slopes are simple no longer. There are clefts, scars, crags, screes, perhaps huge hollow corries you could not see before. And as the sun goes round and probes from different angles you find new gullies, new buttresses being unravelled by the play of light with shadow.

Looking at Snowdonia's skin in this way is altogether fascinating. But no matter how much you admire, describe, dissect, paint or photograph the mountain scene you are still not getting below the skin. Which is what you must do to begin to understand what a mountain really is. You need to go back into the vastness of time past and see how mountains have been made and then destroyed and made again into those we know today.

The geology of North Wales is not easily grasped and anyone unversed in it can be forgiven, as they climb up Snowdon, if they do not at once perceive a crucial fact about this highest peak south of the Grampians: that it was once part of an ocean bed, as is shown by the fossil sea-shells that lie in sedimentary rocks near the summit. But these shells and sediments are less than half the story. For the bulk of the mountain is made of hard volcanic material. So Snowdon's rocks are a real oddity and the only explanation for such a hugger-mugger is that it all resulted from submarine eruptions. We can picture sedimentation taking place on the ancient ocean bed: fragments of detritus and shells settling down to a great thickness and consolidating at last into rocks and fossils. Then this quiet process is disturbed by ocean-bed volcanoes which spread ash and lava across the ocean floor. The eruptions cease and sedimentation continues for another unimaginable lapse of time, burying the volcanic rocks. But other periods of vulcanicity

come along, followed by other times when the volcanoes are quietly buried.

The result over the 50 million years of Ordovician time was a huge build-up of alternating layers of sedimentary and volcanic rock. Ultimately these were uplifted to form dry land, were crumpled by the built-in tensions of the earth's crust into upfolds and downfolds, and have ever since been eroded until they have become what we know today as the mountains and valleys of Snowdonia. It is a landscape formed mainly of hard peaks of igneous rock that look at each other across deep wide gulfs where softer, sedimentary rocks have dissolved and gone down the rivers.

So, if you are a mountaineer, you can follow the curve of the Horseshoe from the resistant lavas of Snowdon to the granitic top of Crib Goch. From there you can scramble down to Pen-y-pass and up the daunting steeps of Glyder Fawr and Glyder Fach on whose tops you will find strange collections of huge, square-edged slabs that at first sight might appear to be the collapsed monuments of an ancient civilisation. They are in fact naturally placed slabs of lava, the debris of a peak long since eroded. Their square corners, straight edges and smooth hard faces speak of the pressures that have split them. Geologists call the process 'jointing' and where such jointed rocks still hold their places in the crags they form cliffs that present climbers with some of their most challenging problems.

The chasm of the Devil's Kitchen (Twll Du) is a perfect example of jointing. From up there you look down into Cwm Idwal, one of Britain's text-book corries. Note the lake and its surround of moraines. They, like the corrie, its rugged cliffs and the scratched rocks all round, are still so eloquent of the age of glaciers that it seems hardly credible that 10,000 years have passed since ice of vast thickness lay there while glaciers were gouging, smoothing and straightening Nant Ffrancon and Llanberis Pass,

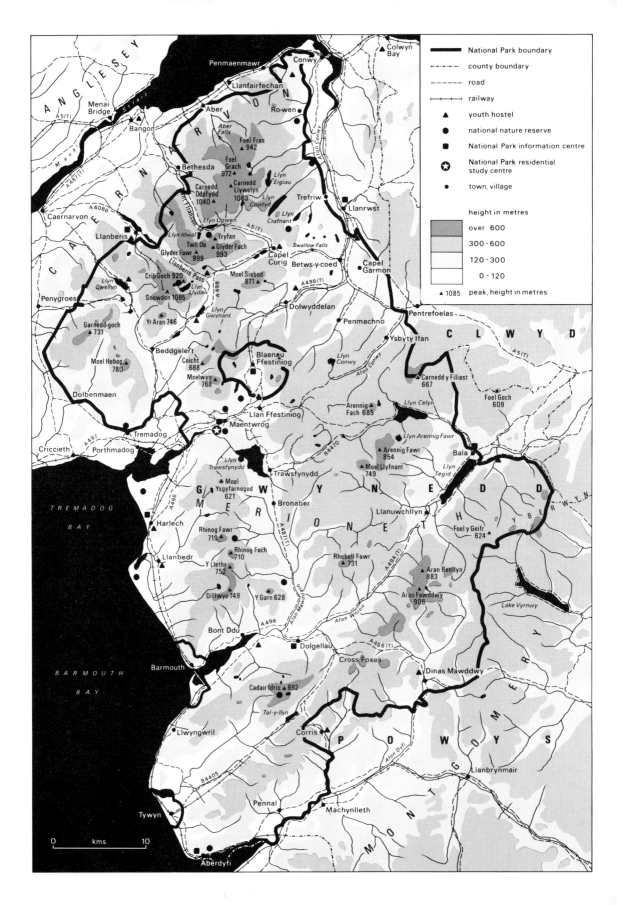

National Park boundary
county boundary
road
railway
▲ youth hostel
● national nature reserve
■ National Park information centre
✪ National Park residential study centre
• town, village

height in metres
over 600
300 - 600
120 - 300
0 - 120
▲1085 peak, height in metres

ANGLESEY

Menai Bridge
Bangor
Caernarvon
Llanberis
Penygroes
Dolbenmaen
Criccieth
Tremadog
Porthmadog
Harlech
Llanbedr
Llwyngwril
Tywyn
Barmouth
Aberdyfi

Penmaenmawr
Conwy
Colwyn Bay
Llanfairfechan
Aber
Ro-wen
Aber Falls
Foel Fras 942
Foel Grach 972
Carnedd Llywelyn 1063
Bethesda
Carnedd Dafydd 1040
Llyn Eigiau
Llyn Cowlyd
Trefriw
Llanrwst
Llyn Crafnant
Llyn Conwy
Llyn Ogwen
Llyn Idwal
Tryfan
Twll Du
Glyder Fach 993
Glyder Fawr 999
Swallow Falls
Capel Curig
Betws-y-coed
Capel Garmon
Crib Goch 920
Llyn Llydaw
Snowdon 1085
Moel Siabod 871
Llanberis Pass
Llyn Cwellyn
Yr Aran 746
Llyn Gwynant
Dolwyddelan
Penmachno
Pentrefoelas
CLWYD
Garnedd-goch 731
Beddgelert
Cnicht 688
Moelwyn 768
Blaenau Ffestiniog
Ysbyty Ifan
Carnedd y Filiast 667
Foel Goch 609
Moel Hebog 780
Llan Ffestiniog
Maentwrog
Llyn Conwy
Arennig Fach 685
Llyn Arennig Fawr
Llyn Trawsfynydd
Trawsfynydd
Arennig Fawr 854
Moel Llyfnant 749
Bala
Llyn Tegid
TREMADOG BAY
Moel Ysgyfarnogod 621
Bronaber
MERIONETH
Llanuwchllyn
Foel y Geifr 624
Rhinog Fawr 719
Rhinog Fach 710
Rhobell Fawr 731
Aran Benllyn 883
Y Llethr 752
Aran Fawddwy 906
Lake Vyrnwy
Diffwys 749
Y Garn 628
Bont Ddu
Dolgellau
Cross Foxes
Dinas Mawddwy
BARMOUTH BAY
Cadair Idris 892
Tal-y-llyn
Corris
POWYS
Pennal
Machynlleth
Llanbrynmair
MONTGOMERY

CAERNARVON

GWYNEDD

CLWYD

BERWYN

A5(T)
A487(T)
A4086
A4085
A5(T)
A496(T)
A498
A470
A494(T)
A496
A458(T)
A487(T)
A497
B4405

0   kms   10

leaving the mouths of tributary valleys hanging in space on either side.

Follow the easy slope from Cwm Idwal down to Ogwen, glancing up on your right at the grim acid lavas of Tryfan. Then across the main road and up more steeps to the summits of the high Carneddau. More massive sheets of volcanic rock underfoot. Descend the great tilted grasslands, find a way past Craig yr Ysfa (note the fine jointing exposed in Great Gully) and so down into the splendours of Cwm Eigiau, finest of all Carneddau valleys: you will have come down through an igneous landscape all the way.

Edge south to other mountain groups. Go clattering up through abandoned slate quarries on Moel Siabod to reach a dolerite summit that looks to the neighbouring igneous heights of Cnicht and Moelwyn. Think, looking across the hollow land, how all this was once a high plateau that, except for the hardest peaks, is now almost gnawed away and is still dissolving. Go right across the park: in any direction you can relate the scenery to the rocks. In the east you will come up to the twin peaks of Arennig: they too are just within the igneous region. South of them stretches another volcanic feature, what we might call the Great Rift Valley of Snowdonia—the thirty-mile line along which all rocks have fractured and slipped sideways to form what geologists know as the Bala fault. It divides Arennig from Berwyn, contains Llyn Tegid, Wales' largest natural lake, passes north of the Aran range (more volcanics) and continues on to the west coast by way of Cross Foxes and Tal-y-llyn pass.

So you come to that well loved mountain Cadair Idris which defies the north and the frosts with magnificent granitic brows, that sometimes seem like a great wave turned to stone just as it was about to break across the Mawddach estuary. From Cadair Idris you look north-west to yet another mountain group—the alluring heights called Diffwys, Llethr and Rhinog. And they are of rocks even older than most of the rest of Snowdonia for they are hard sedimentary material of Cambrian age and were not laid bare until thousands of feet of Silurian and Ordovician material had been eroded from over them. The Rhinog range, especially in its northern half, offers you as much bare rock, hard going and solitude as you will meet with anywhere in Snowdonia.

Grey rocks, brown rocks, rocks red with iron, streaks of quartz gleaming silver in the sun, dolerites that are nearly black: all give something to the mountain scene. But even in upland Snowdonia bare rock, truly bare rock, doesn't amount to much in the total landscape. Develop a botanist's eye for rock and you'll see how very often it owes its greens, its yellows, its pallor, its blackness entirely to the lichens that cover it.

Grasslands that are green in summer and fade to light straw-colour in winter cover almost all the better-drained shoulders and slopes of the hills. Countless millions of leaves of grass: yet their species are extremely few. Take away sheep's fescue, common bent and mat-grass and what have you left? In autumn richly russet patches show where cotton sedge, common rush and purple moor-grass are changing colour on tussocky, ankle-testing peat moors. Beside them those dark stretches, almost black in winter light, are where the peat has gone under heather. Another black or dark green mantle is a block of Sitka or other spruces, plantings that may be enlivened here and there by stripes of larch that come bright green in spring, warmly red in winter.

Many slopes below 1,600ft are dense with bracken. Dark green in summer they go brown in autumn, a brown that can become a fiery red if caught by a setting winter sun. Frost-tender, bracken cannot get a footing in the colder uplands, but at lower heights it is reckoned to have spread enormously in the past century or two as cattle have yielded place to sheep. For cattle trample young bracken and discourage it, but sheep step lightly between the uncurling fronds and allow them to grow into a jungle. No farm animals eat bracken. Not even goats. But herbicides to tackle bracken are now being developed and the next few years could well give us back green grassy slopes where bracken once spread widely.

The bracken zone is also that of the sessile oak which, like bracken, thrives best on well drained slopes. The valleyside oakwoods, often only small patches or narrow tongues, are the descendants of the natural forest we can suppose occupied much of lowland and semi-upland Snowdonia until about the end of the Dark Ages. Since then farmlands have been liberally sliced out of the forest and the woods that survive are mostly tolerated as a source of fencing posts and for the shelter they give stock in bad weather. Constantly grazed they seldom have any understorey of shrubs or wildflowers; and you hardly ever find a young oak in them. They are not woodlands so much as pastures with trees. And lacking regeneration they must eventually disappear unless taken in hand before it's too late. Those few Snowdonian oakwoods that are protected as nature reserves and are rich in wildlife, are splendid examples of what could be done to conserve the rest.

You will not go much about the hills without observing that the vegetation is of two sorts. There are the smotherers—grassland, heather, cotton sedge, bilberry, deer grass and similar empire-seekers. And there are the plants that grow discreetly here and there, holding to their modest places in the world with little sign of territorial ambition. To the average amateur plant-seeker it is these unsprawling species that are by far the most endearing. For often he finds them growing in each other's company in great

variety. To see these choicer species you must make your way to those rare places that even the most irrepressible smotherers have not conquered. And the best of such localities are those dripping, lime-rich, soft-rock ledges of high-altitude crags that face north or east where the droughts of spring or summer (yes, even Snowdon has its droughts) cannot harm them.

Up there grows the purple saxifrage whose mass of showy flowers may startle you amid the north winds and icicles of Easter. Purple saxifrage blooms alone when its neighbours are still in winter sleep. But in due time they all appear and if you explore the high corries round Snowdon, Glyder and the Carneddau you will surely discover at least the commoner ones in their season: moss campion, mountain sorrel, mossy saxifrage, starry saxifrage, snowy saxifrage; the tiny, delectable Snowdon lily not found elsewhere in Britain; alpine meadow-rue; arctic chickweed; alpine scurvy-grass; alpine saw-wort; chickweed willow herb; three-flowered rush. Or by diligence or good fortune you might come upon some of Snowdonia's rarer ones: mountain avens, northern rock cress, twisted whitlow-grass, alpine chickweed, alpine cinquefoil, hair-sedge, alpine meadow-grass and several others. Holly fern and the two woodsia ferns also survive in the mountain rocks although they were mercilessly collected by nineteenth-century fern trowels.

That many of these plants belong more properly to Europe's coldest regions adds vastly to the fascination of finding them in Snowdonia. Here they must be regarded as a group with a past rather than a future. Our age, it seems fair to suppose, is set in the tail end of a glacial period, and our arctic-alpine plants are the survivors of a far richer alpine flora that once

Looking down the Pass of Llanberis from Crib Goch; the high igneous peaks of Snowdonia are separated by long glaciated valleys occupied by rivers and lakes

flourished here but which has largely given up the struggle against our uncertain summers and against winters that are an uneasy alternation of mild spells and cold snaps—not at all the conditions enjoyed by typical alpines.

So although it looks as if Snowdonia's relict community of arctic-alpines, the most southerly of any importance in Britain, is doomed to eventual extinction (unless another Ice Age comes along in time to save them) there is a more cheering side of the region's flora. The conditions so harrowing for arctic-alpines are just what many temperate-climate species revel in. So joyously up the mountains they have gone, lots of lowlanders formerly kept down in the valleys by the frosty breath of glaciers. You will find golden rod, ox-eye daisy, globe flower, lady's smock, birdsfoot trefoil, wild strawberry, wild angelica, primrose, meadowsweet, slender St John's wort, yellow pimpernel, self-heal, harebell and many others, all flourishing abundantly, full of green and sappy growth, enjoying life along the mountain ledges in the company of the remaining arctic-alpines. Below the mountain zone there are many other good places for the plant-seeker in Snowdonia—damp, base-rich meadows, for instance, with their orchids and sedges, or shadowed stream gorges quite green with ferns and mosses. Or the fine dunes of Harlech and Dyffryn, both national nature reserves which are rich in orchids and coastal species.

As for the park's animals and birds it is surely the survival here of a wealth of predators that is most distinctive. With its uplands largely houseless and even its valleys, most of them, thinly populated, Snowdonia is a region where human pressure on wildlife has been less severe than in much of Europe. Gamekeepers, for instance, are few. And the farmers on the whole are fairly tolerant of predators except the fox. The abundance of buzzards alone is proof enough of this. The position of the peregrine is not so cheerful; this fine bird is still deplorably scarce, though elsewhere in Britain its numbers are slowly recovering from the insecticide disaster of several years ago.

Among predatory mammals the fox, despite intense persecution, survives amazingly. Badgers, stoats, weasels are also common enough. Otters though diminishing are not yet rare. Polecats have greatly increased this century which makes the failure of the marten to do likewise rather a mystery. Once widespread it must now be regarded as very rare. For the red squirrel too, a dismal report. As the grey squirrel rampaged through east and south Wales during the last twenty years Snowdonia long held out as a refuge for the red. But now even here the defences are down and the grey is nearly everywhere triumphant. To see a red squirrel today your best hope is probably to visit oak woodland at the heads of valleys; or look in upland conifer plantations.

Some of the birds of prey have already been mentioned. For the park's other birds you can choose between the estuaries with their shelducks, wigeon, mergansers and waders; or the oakwoods with their redstarts, pied flycatchers and wood warblers; or you can go for the upland birds. But remember that birds in all mountain regions become scarcer the further up you go, and also that like the choicest plants, the choicest birds are restricted to special places. Wheatears are mostly on screes; common sandpipers at stony streamsides and lake edges; dippers and grey wagtails by waterfalls or rapids; red grouse up on the heather moors; black grouse round the edges of young forestry plantations; ring ouzels in small heathery crags; peregrines and ravens along the greater cliffs; choughs near old mine shafts and quarries. Away from these particular localities you can walk for miles, even in spring and summer, across the wide grassy places of the hills and see no birds but meadow pipits and skylarks. In winter you may find no birds at all.

Fish are important in Snowdonia. For though there aren't many species there is distinct quality about the few that do swim in the cold depths of the lakes or in the green pools of the rivers. In a few lakes there are char, a rather mysterious fish because it comes up into shallow water only to breed towards the year's end. Even less known is the gwyniad, a species of the whitefish group: it lives in Llyn Tegid at Bala and nowhere else, a deep-water fish to be taken only in nets for it scorns all anglers' lures. Char and gwyniad can be thought of along with arctic-alpine plants: they are relics of colder days. In mountain streams you will see plenty of darting troutlets that can never hope to grow big in the clear rocky waters because the fish food is swept away by one spate after another throughout the year. Some of the rivers such as Dyfi, Mawddach, Dwyryd and Conwy are famous for salmon and sea trout: and these big migrants can go far into the inhospitable upland reaches because once they have quit the sea they require no more food till they are back in the salt again. The only water in the park that has a good variety of fish is Llyn Tegid: it owes its perch, its roach, its pike, its grayling, to the fact that it alone among Snowdonia's lakes is linked with lowland England—by the Dee that flows down into Cheshire.

Perhaps, looking across the quiet uplands from some prominent height, you may wonder how natural they are. The vast sheep-dotted grasslands climbing, dipping and rolling to far horizons, how near are they to being what ecologists call primary grasslands; grasslands, that is, that were there before man interfered? And when did man begin to change the Snowdonian scene? All indications are that he was a late-comer here. The vast reaches both of Paleolithic and Mesolithic time seem to have come and gone without man having any busi-ness to attend to in Snowdonia.

So we come to the Neolithic or New Stone Age which began in North Wales about 3300 BC. To see something tangible surviving from that shadowy world you should find your way up the winding lanes from Betws-y-coed to the well restored chambered tomb at Capel Garmon that looks across the wide Conwy valley and away to the high Carneddau. But it will speak to you chiefly of death rather than life. There are other tombs from that far-off time. There is Maen-y-bardd, for instance, where great stones mark an ancient road a mile west of Ro-wen, and the village of Dyffryn Ardudwy boasts a pair of graves. Best of all, because they still retain something of their ancient covering of boulders, are the fine chambered tombs of Carneddau Hengwm near Barmouth.

Neolithic man, we can fairly say, did two things for the land we call Snowdonia. His first accomplishment, as a migrant from Europe, was to set up the pioneer cultural links between North Wales and the Continent, links he ex-tended to Ireland. Second, by bringing with him cattle (the original Welsh blacks?), sheep and seed corn, he initiated farming here. Not that he ever seriously penetrated Snowdonia's uplands: the climate was too hostile. So we find his chambered tombs are nearly all coastal or not far above sea level. He was ingenious: look-ing for tool-making materials he discovered he could shape and sharpen the igneous rocks around Penmaenmawr into implements like those made from flints in eastern England. These he evidently used as axes for felling trees and as mattocks for breaking the soil. But tools like this were not all that effective and perhaps the hands to wield them were not very many. So it seems safe to assume that Neolithic man never cleared whole forests or created great fields.

But times and people were to change. By about 1800 BC the Continent was sending us its

73

next wave of immigrants, the so-called Beaker people who were the heralds of the Bronze Age. They came at an enviable period, climatically. Presumably the Azores anticyclone took a step northwards and for maybe a thousand years caressed north-west Europe with calmer, warmer, drier weather than had gone before or has happened since. By the evidence of pollen analysis we know that there was a drying-up of mountain bogs and that oaks advanced into the hills, and inevitably the tide of human life followed. Many Bronze Age tools and weapons have been found in highland Snowdonia; ancient trackways have been traced across, perhaps making for southern England as trade routes; burial cairns stand on many a mountain top.

After this halcyon spell of sub-boreal climate north-west Europe once more found itself in the path of storms and depressions, the Snowdonian uplands became increasingly uninhabitable, the bogs returned, the trees withdrew and the next immigrants, the Iron Age people, built their forts on the foothills not on the mountains. Within the park itself the Iron Age has left little that is impressive. There is nothing, for example, to compare with Tre'r Ceiri, the splendid walled town full of hut foundations on Yr Eifl not far outside the western border of the park. Still, there are a few notable hill forts like that of Craig y Dinas ('Crag of the Fortress') that stands above the Ysgethin stream near Dyffryn Ardudwy. It is a place worth visiting not only for this jauntily perched fort which still retains some of its walled defences but also for the tract it overlooks. There are wild rough pastures divided by long drystone walls and wilderness areas of scattered rocks. Stony-edged lakes squat at the feet of empty hills while a few scattered cairns of the Bronze Age and chambered tombs of the Stone Age remain to give this whole district the feeling of a prehistoric landscape strangely preserved, unaltered by the passage of the years.

So around 500 BC, at a time of awful climate, the Iron Age and the Celts arrived. Their coming was crucial for Snowdonia and all Wales. For though during the succeeding centuries the Celts of most of England were gradually driven west or absorbed by Romans, Saxons, Danes, Normans and others, the Celts of Wales have survived remarkably and so has their pre-Roman language which you will hear spoken throughout the region.

In contrast the impact of the Romans on Snowdonia, though doubtless sharp while it lasted, seems to have left few enduring effects on society. Their military presence is of some topographical interest in that their main road linking three important forts at Caerhun, Trawsfynydd and Pennal makes a neat north-south axis down the centre of the park. This road is crossed equally neatly in the centre of the park near Trawsfynydd by an east-west axis formed by the line of a trackway (probably Bronze Age) which links the ancient ports of Llanbedr and Harlech with the east and south.

With the Dark Ages we find the earliest Christians, missionaries who, entering Wales by western sea-routes from the fifth century onwards, travelled through the country spreading the new religion. Their connections being strongly with Ireland, Cornwall and Brittany they did much to keep the Celtic tradition alive. They had Celtic names like Curig, Cadfan and Tannwg. Some of the places where they settled and preached were long kept sacred, eventually becoming the sites of medieval churches, some of whose ancient buildings still survive. Go, for instance, to Llanrhychwyn on its shelf above the Conwy valley near Llanrwst. Or to old Llangelynnin church eight miles north. You don't need to be a Christian to be moved by these simple old buildings in their lonely settings; by their roof-timbers of local oak; by the stonework of their thick walls; by the long

Snowdonia is particularly popular with fell walkers and is rich in natural history. There are still many arctic-alpine plants which are unique at this latitude and the area has seen the resurgence of such species as the buzzard and the badger. Snowdonia is of great importance to the conservationist

history of their sites.

Harlech castle, so firm upon its sea-commanding bastion of Cambrian rock, is Snowdonia's most famous reminder of medieval days. A symbol of English power in the thirteenth century, it was also probably a link between Ireland and England. From Harlech a road climbed inland to Cwm Bychan then slipped through the hostile rocks of Rhinog by way of a carefully paved staircase that still survives, the misnamed Roman Steps. Using the pass of Bwlch Tyddiad men and pack horses went swiftly east to Bala, then a key place on the road towards London. That the English felt no need to build a great castle at Bala indicates their greater confidence on that side of Snowdonia compared with their nervousness in the more dangerous west. The rest of the Middle Ages survives in other castles such as that of Dinas Emrys near Beddgelert, the high-placed ruins of Dolwyddelan, and Castell y Bere near Tywyn. Elsewhere there are castle mounds without castles: many of them speak of the bloody side of life at a period even earlier than

The national parks are popular both with motorists and with
coach parties but rarely is the road as free from traffic

that of most stone castles. Pathetic stumps of walls near Dolgellau are all that is left of the once powerful Cistercian abbey of Cymer.

Snowdonia is not famed for domestic architecture. To the threshold of our own time most people here have lived the hard way, wrenching a poor existence out of unkind soils on the farms or from hostile rocks in the quarries. And elegance has been far from their thoughts. So the villages of dark stone, roofed over with sombre slate and dominated by huge austere chapels, reflect perfectly the severity that produced them. Most of the farmhouses are better.

Standing alone, they often have spaciousness, sometimes shapeliness, and are frequently perfectly placed. Often they sit on just the right shelf with grey rocks and yellow gorse all round, a hurrying mountain stream below, a tremendous, hawthorn-scattered hillside above, a few weather-battered sycamores or Scots pines sheltering them on either side. The lichened outbuildings, often far, far older than the house, have immensely thick walls made with rough boulders, which, together with ancient oak beams, proclaim a style primitive enough to have come from medieval times.

Should you find house and outbuildings standing in one long line then you may well have discovered a descendant of the traditional Celtic long house.

Metals are widespread in Snowdonia's rocks and have perhaps been mined since pre-Roman days. There are old copper mines east and west of Snowdon and on the mountain itself. Another copper belt with a little gold and lead in it stretches from Bont Ddu on the Mawddach estuary north-east to Rhobell Fawr. Iron has been worked on a small scale at several places and manganese mines penetrate the Cambrian rocks of Rhinog. All these ores are low-grade and have long been regarded as uneconomic. But today, with new technology available for exploiting ores of poor yield and with generous government aid as an added incentive, mining companies are again taking an interest in Snowdonia. The region's rocks have long been worked for slate but today this is decreasing. Roadstone comes largely from quarries of granite and dolerite.

Snowdonia lives largely by sheep, cattle and tourism. But these industries, together with other employments, cannot provide work for all who seek it. Inevitably, like rural areas the world over, Snowdonia exports people, especially young people, to far-away towns. And though the farms are prosperous and the farming future looks bright, the remoter villages are declining as more and more of their houses become holiday cottages that are closed and dismal all winter and whose summer occupants are in the village but not of it. Some of the bigger, less remote villages fare better and are increasing. But too often this increase is effected by tacking on an unimaginative block of council houses, unattractive both in design and materials.

What of the future of Snowdonia and its National Park? There are questions that urgently need an answer. Is mining, for instance, to be allowed and if so on what scale? Should any other heavy industries be admitted? Are conifers to go on spreading? When are we to get a policy aimed at conserving what is left of the deciduous woodland?

And what about the problems of tourism as more and more visitors crowd in along high-speed roads from populous England? Not every tourist wants a quiet walk across the hills and nothing more. Between them tourists want hotels and caravans, scenic roads and rough tracks for car rallies and motorbike scrambles, more and more places to fish, to birdwatch, to ride, lakes for yachting and water-skiing—the list is endless. Some want to build houses as second homes or as places for their retirement or simply to make money.

The total demand is a heavy one on so small and vulnerable a region, and conflicts are inevitable. Conflict between ramblers and farmers; between those for and against the holiday cottage movement; between Welsh nationalists and English tourists. Mining, reservoirs, power stations, all have their critics.

There is also a strong-voiced lobby against conifer forests. But a signpost into the future is that there are plans to use them to absorb a multitude of people and cars. The intention is to encourage touring motorists to get off the roads into generous car parks and picnicking places. There will be information kiosks and from them walking trails will lead off through the forest to camp sites, viewpoints and other places of interest. Provision will be made for pony trekking, caravanning, boating and fishing. There will be shops, restaurants and log cabins. Even the forests themselves could slowly improve if the present spruce crop, as it matures, is replaced here and there by species that would break up the heavy black blanket of the forests of today. And much could be done to make sections of the forests into really good nature reserves.

77

But though the new-look forestry policy seems to offer some hope to tourists it is difficult to see Snowdonia's other problems being solved. The basic trouble is that we in Britain have never yet got clear in our minds just what a national park is for, how and by whom it should be administered, and how far its natural resources should or should not be exploited by industry, farming or tourism. Until these crucial issues are sorted out, until some philosophy of the whole countryside, including national parks, has evolved, then regions like Snowdonia will go on being the scene of squalid arguments. And we shall continue as we are now, never knowing from one day to the next what new monstrosity will threaten us in the shape of some chalet park staged conspicuously up a hillside; or an opencast mine ripping up square miles of the mountains; or an atomic power station set with the grossest incongruity on a lonely moorland; or yet another deciduous woodland being cleared for Sitka spruces. Snowdonia is one of the highest quality areas of Britain. It deserves a better fate than to be thrown to the Philistines and the speculators, or to be haggled over for ever by politicians.

For the past two centuries people have been singing the praises of Snowdonia. So for anyone with a taste for past writings there is a vast literature to be explored, beginning with Thomas Pennant's leisurely and erudite *Tours in Wales* which contains what is still a most readable account of his journeys to Snowdon in the 1770s. Some of the more recent books are indicated in the bibliography. In addition there are periodicals such as *Archaeologia Cambrensis*, *Nature in Wales* and other specialised journals in which Snowdonia is frequently mentioned.

But reading is only one way of finding out. Getting to know the people is another, and the many people who live and work in Snowdonia will give you information and points of view you will not find written anywhere. Then, armed with all you have read and heard you can go out into the hills and valleys of Snowdonia and make your own interpretations of the scene, judge for yourself the opinions that have been voiced and enjoy in your own way what is a quite unique and delightful corner of the world.

One final point: Snowdonia should as far as possible be explored on foot. A car is not only a monstrous intrusion into the wilder places, it also deprives the traveller of the correct perspective. The scene before him should unfold slowly, revealing its charms and secrets gently so that they can be really appreciated. Snowdonia is rich in footpaths: they go up to all summits, they cross ridges from valley to valley, they link everywhere with everywhere. They are waiting for you.

Chapter 6

PEAK DISTRICT

Patrick Monkhouse

AREA: *542 square miles* (*140,378ha*)
ALTITUDE: *318 – 2,088ft* (*97 – 637m*)
        Kinder Scout 2,088ft (*637m*)
        Bleaklow Head 2,060ft (*628m*)
ADMINISTRATION: *The Peak District National Park Joint Planning Board has 33 members of whom 22 are appointed by the 6 constituent County Councils and includes 4 members representing the 9 District Councils. Derbyshire County Council has 8 representatives, the County Councils of Staffordshire and Cheshire 2 each, and the Metropolitan County Councils of Greater Manchester, West Yorkshire and South Yorkshire 2 each. 11 members are appointed by the Secretary of State for the Environment.*
POPULATION: *44,000. Bakewell, 4,240; Hathersage, 1,522.*
COMMUNICATIONS: *Close to the national park there are main line stations at Sheffield, Chesterfield and Macclesfield, and other stations at Buxton and Matlock.*

   By road Sheffield to Bakewell is 17 miles; Manchester – Castleton 28 miles; Ashbourne – Newhaven 10 miles.

   A British Rail service runs from Sheffield to stations at Grindleford, Hathersage, Hope and Edale in the park.

   There are many privately operated bus services and ones sponsored by the Peak Board.
VIEWPOINTS *with or near car parks:*
Carl Wark (*SK 260815*)
Cat and Fiddle (*SK 002710*)
Froggatt Edge (*SK 251765*)
Longstone Edge (*SK 201729*)
Monsal Head (*SK 185715*)
NATIONAL PARK INFORMATION CENTRES:
Bakewell. The Market Hall, Bridge Street; tel Bakewell 3227 (*SK 217265*)
Buxton. St Ann's Well, The Crescent; tel Buxton 2060 (*SK 058735*)
Castleton. Castle Street; tel Hope 679 (*SK 150828*)
Edale. Field Head; tel Edale 207 (*SK 124856*)
Mobile.
OTHER VISITOR CENTRES, MUSEUMS:
Bakewell. Old House Museum (*SK 215686*)
Chatsworth. Farming and Forestry Exhibition (*SK 263704*)
NATIONAL PARK RESIDENTIAL STUDY CENTRE, *Losehill Hall, Castleton, Sheffield S30 2WB*
NATIONAL PARK OFFICER, *National Park Office, Baslow Road, Bakewell, Derbyshire DE4 1AE*

The Peak is the most southerly part of the Pennine Chain, the last forty miles or so of hilly country before the long ridge running from the Cheviots and the Scottish Border sinks into the plains of the Midlands. In a way it is the epitome of this great range, recalling and summing up in itself the chain's essential features, its imposing elegance, its alternation of light and dark.

   The hill country, some of the most beautiful in England, is of two strongly contrasting kinds:

sombre lonely uncultivated moors with walls of dark stone and peat-covered summits that run to around 2,000ft above precipitous scarps and broad valleys, and bright, green upland pastures, enclosed by light-coloured walls, with white crags and steep-sided gorges, and lovely wooded dales. They are often distinguished as the Dark Peak and the White Peak. The Dark Peak based on gritstone lies north, with narrowing belts in the west and east; the limestone, which fills the bulk of the south, makes up the White Peak. Although the Peak never rises as high as the northern Pennines, it commands its own scales and proportions, and can be imposing and exquisite by turn.

Besides its natural beauty, the Peak has, as a national park, another virtue. It is situated where it is most needed. No one needs access to natural beauty so much as those who live perforce in large industrial towns. With Sheffield and Manchester, Derby and Stoke-on-Trent on its borders, the Peak welcomes the country-goer who has neither time nor money for long journeys or long holidays. Many of those who come to it show their appreciation by serving as unpaid wardens on the moors over which the Peak Park Planning Board has negotiated access agreements with the landowners. At the other extreme you will find the wardens at work over new routes like the Tissington Trail, once a railway line, today a footpath and pony-trekking trail with a wide outlook over the surrounding country and with many features of botanical interest, now looked after on behalf of the Peak Board by the Derbyshire Naturalists' Trust.

The Peak was the first national park designated in Britain. It came into being on 15 November 1951. It was a bold beginning, being by no means the easiest or the most obvious place in which to make a start on a new and untried system. It was, for a national park, quite heavily populated, with more than 40,000 people living in it and with substantial industries (quarrying, cement making, textiles, plastics) already on the ground, in sharp contrast with the many miles of uninhabited moorland and lonely farmsteads. Many of its rivers were dammed to make reservoirs supplying 4 million people with water. Great cities pressed on its flanks. Its boundaries were drawn to take in parts of five counties (including Sheffield County Borough). It was a complex structure for a social experiment. No other park was defined with more than three partners; and now the Peak, after the local government reorganisation of 1974, has six.

But there were good reasons for starting with the Peak. Its natural beauties were perhaps under greater threat of ill-considered industrial action than in any other embryo national park: and it had on its borders more people well placed (and accustomed) to enjoy it.

The beauties of the Peak, while rarely tremendous in the way that Scafell and Snowdon, drawing much of their raw material from their volcanic past, can be tremendous, are subtly impressive. Their music is in a different key. Carboniferous Limestone, Millstone Grit and the shale grit which often lies between them form hills which, although often striking, are of only moderate height; even Kinder Scout, the highest point, would be inconspicuous if transferred to North Wales or to the Lakes.

Like most of the Pennine range the Peak is made almost wholly of sedimentary rocks, not all of one kind but all laid down little by little on prehistoric sea-floors or marshes, and brought to their present shape and height millions of years later by water and ice and subterranean pressures. There are some rocks of volcanic origin in the Peak (known as 'toadstone') but they are relatively slight and inconspicuous, mere intrusions into the massive sediments peacefully accumulating under water.

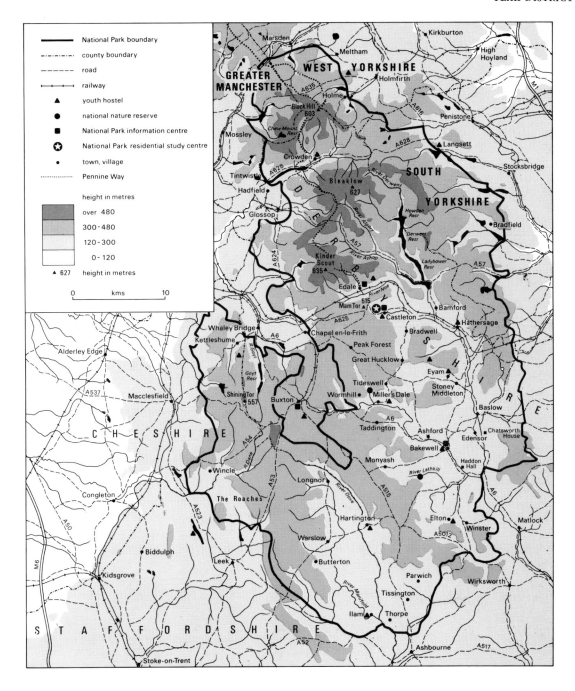

Its name has puzzled many of those who have visited it, and who recall Dr Johnson's definition of a peak as 'a sharply pointed hill'. Such peaks are rare in the Peak, and its highest hill, Kinder Scout, is about the flattest-topped mountain in Britain. But the name has really nothing to do with pointed hills. At some time in the Middle Ages, it was inhabited by a tribe known as the

Peacs. Their home was naturally called Peac-land: and when they died and were forgotten, the name survived in the misleading form of Peakland, presently shortened to the Peak.

But if the Peak has no Pillar Rock or Lliwedd, it makes good use of its own kinds of rock. The Millstone Grit is a fine hard rock, not merely sustaining the higher moors but also forming some remarkable crags, though not of any great height. There are fine examples all along the chain of 'Edges' which flank the River Derwent on the east, and the Peak's best known water-fall (Kinder Downfall) leaps over a wall of grit-stone on the west face of Kinder Scout.

You see no waterfalls in the White Peak, the limestone country, which forms so much of the southern part of the National Park, because the water eats the limestone away and leaves itself nothing to tumble over. Instead, water running over limestone tends to excavate deep and nar-row gorges, thus creating what are to many people the most attractive spectacles of the Peak: the famous ten miles or so of Dovedale between Hartington and Thorpe Cloud, or the companion piece on the River Manifold, a few miles east of Dovedale. Cheedale in the upper Wye valley, which is overlooked by the massive white buttress of Chee Tor, is another good example, as is the dry valley (for the water flows most of the way underground) which runs down from the village of Peak Forest to Miller's Dale (known successively as Dame Dale, Hay Dale, Peter Dale and Monk's Dale).

There are other variations on the limestone-and-water theme. The water may sink into a crack in the rock, work its way down, dissolve the underlying limestone and hollow out a cave. The Peak Cavern at Castleton is the most celebrated of these (in part, no doubt, because it has now an imposing entrance as well as a lengthy underground fissure). But something like fifty of these stream-fissures are known in the Peak, some of them discovered by the lead miners. The Peak's two pot-holes, Eldon Hole and Nettle Pot, are vertical versions of this same phenomenon.

The third main component of the Peak is the shale grit, the end-product of a prehistoric mud which, though being less resistant than the Mill-stone Grit and consequently more easily disinte-grated and washed away, has left steep slopes often crowned or interspersed with gritstone. The upper Derwent valley with its reservoirs, the Ashop valley which joins it, the Mam Tor ridge south of Edale, are all examples of the shale grit country. Kinder Scout, or rather its upper plateau, is a long block of Millstone Grit, lying on a pedestal of shale grit, which gives Kinder its steep sides. Bleaklow, the next hill to the north, is pretty well all gritstone, and this continues to the northern boundary of the National Park, except for the Etherow valley with its chain of reservoirs. Here the river has cut its way down to reveal the underlying shale grit for a stretch of three or four miles on the floor of the valley.

Out of this rock sandwich—gritstone lying on shale lying on limestone—the Peak eventu-ally emerged. But not yet! Before that, all these rocks were buried under a further series of marine deposits now wholly vanished. Then earth movements rumpled the surface as it then was, throwing up a long fold along the line which is now the ridge of the Pennines. More millions of years wore away this upper land, leaving nothing of it but the pattern of its rivers which, as it wore away, it transferred to the older underlying rocks as they re-emerged, to carve out in their own good time the basic pattern of the Peak we know.

The basic pattern—yes. But only the basis. When gritstone disintegrates it becomes a sandy or gravelly sort of soil; the heavy rainfall tends to wash out soluble material, leaving barren boggy stuff and it is this that covers the peaty moorlands on the top of Kinder Scout and

The old Buxton railway track has been transformed by the Peak Park Planning Board for those on foot and on horseback. The Tissington Trail is an example of imaginative planning by a park authority

Bleaklow. They were not always so bare. There is evidence (largely from ancient pollen found in the peat) that some 8,000 years ago these hills were clothed in birch forest, which extended over much of the Peak District. That this has disappeared is due in part to changes in climate, in part to the intervention of man, both in felling trees in prehistoric times, and, in relatively recent times, using the local timber (for lack of local coal) for the smelting of lead.

Happily there has lately been some recovery,

though in the valleys rather than on the high moors. Two hundred years ago, Sir Richard Arkwright, while managing his textile mills at Cromford, planted 50,000 trees a year in the Derwent valley. The good work has been continued since his day, partly by the landowners, partly by the reservoir builders, and more recently by the Forestry Commission, and, in sensitive spots, by the Peak Park Planning Board.

A great part of the Peak is, of course, farmed,

83

and skilfully farmed, but for milk and meat and wool rather than for corn or cabbages. Sheep are the mainstay. They are found all over the place; even the high northern moors, where pasture appears very sparse, sustain about two sheep an acre. The characteristic breed is naturally the Derbyshire Gritstone, hornless and speckle-faced; after these, Swaledales, Lonks and Scotch Blackface are the commonest. Cattle, mainly Shorthorns, are pastured over the lower hills—up to about 1,500ft.

Some of the farms have very long histories, going back to the days when they were run in conjunction with the monasteries; these often have the word 'grange' as part of their name. The pastures are marked out with innumerable stone walls. It has been estimated that an average farm of about seventy-five acres or so in five-acre fields will have about three miles of walling.

The pattern of the Peak we know today does not consist only of its natural features. It owes much also to the works of man over the last 6,000 years, as well as to the forces of nature. Many of us, coming from over-inhabited parts of Britain, are drawn towards raw country, the face of nature unmarred by the hand of man. This is indeed an important aspect of national parks. But in all of them, and perhaps especially in the Peak, the works of man have taken on in some degree the character of the country as natural evolution has left it—all but a few indigestible ones, mostly of recent origin, and there is now a curb on these. Elsewhere mankind has added much to the character, even something to the beauty, of the Peak.

This is true particularly of the limestone country, or rather its uplands; one cannot better nature in Dovedale. With the relatively gentle contours of most of the White Peak, and the sparseness of trees there, villages or groups of farm buildings seem often as much in place and as acceptable aesthetically as a natural feature

like a crag or a wood. They seem growing things.

Professor Tarn, in his book *The Peak District National Park—Its Architecture*, makes the point that in the seventeenth century all isolated areas, as the Peak then was, 'soon become full of special local characteristics, the qualities of which we would term style in a more sophisticated context, but which are really little more than idiomatic ways of doing things, standard practices and well proved details, worked out over the years and passed on from father to son, from master craftsman to apprentices'.

The remarkable continuity of the Peak's building tradition is brought out in a chapter (in a guide to the National Park, published a dozen years ago) by Colonel Gerald Haythornthwaite, himself an architect and a leading member of the Peak Park Planning Board:

> Each succeeding age provided its own architectural variations but did not depart from the basic tradition in Peak District building. Haddon Hall, the most interesting and romantic of all the buildings of the Peak, grew slowly over five and a half centuries, passing from its Norman beginnings through all the native phases of architectural style: Early English, Decorated and Perpendicular Gothic, Tudor and early Elizabethan Renaissance ... For each new addition, the builders took advantage of the new thoughts in design and the new methods of construction which were current at the time, but so submitted to the natural conditions of the site that each new part was perfectly related to the existing buildings and to the landscape ... Haddon Hall stands as the exemplar of free architectural development within a relatively unchanging landscape.

But the great houses (Chatsworth and Lyme are the other two) come relatively late. They mark, it may be thought, a climax in the human civilisation of the Peak; much has been added since they were built, little that looks like outlasting them.

The Peak has also a far older pattern of human activity, the relics of which take us back into a remote past and into a human situation now hard to envisage. The country, and especially the great limestone plateau, is dotted with relics of early man, who seems to have been established here as much as 4,000 years ago.

Of his surviving works Arbor Low is the most impressive. It takes us back to the late Neolithic period, or possibly the early Bronze Age. It does not suggest as high a level of human achievement as Stonehenge or Avebury: yet in its own way and in its own setting it is just as impressive. It lies on the limestone plateau a few hundred yards south of the Long Rake, the old road which links Youlgreave to the Roman road (now the A515) from Buxton to Ashbourne. A rough farm lane leads to the Low. A bank, seeming at first sight more a natural than a human feature, conceals, until you are right on it, all but the outer shell of the monument.

From the bank you look down on what, it is supposed, is the shrine: a flat-topped mound of earth surrounded by a 10ft ditch, with two great limestone blocks prone on the mound's top and with forty or more, prone likewise, lying all round. It is hard to judge if they were ever upright.

The date of this work has been put at somewhere between 1700 and 1400 BC. Massive, secretive, in a much higher and bleaker setting than Stonehenge or Avebury, and far less widely known, this gesture made by primitive man in the stern face of nature seems deeply and memorably moving.

There are other stone circles in the Peak— Hob Hurst's House near Baslow, the Eyam Moor circle, and the Nine Ladies near Bakewell. But Arbor Low is the one that matters. After more than 3,000 years, it retains the aura of a sanctuary.

From the Iron Age there survive numerous hill forts; notably on Mam Tor, where the rampart is conspicuous across the valley; on Combs Moss, overlooking Chapel-en-le-Frith; and per-haps Carl Wark ('Churls' Work') on Hathersage Moor, though there is some uncertainty about the date of this.

The Romans, as always, left their mark upon the Peak, though there is no evidence of a large Roman population here. The curative waters of Buxton seem to have been known to them (under the name of *Aquae Arnametiae*) and they are known to have got lead from the Peak. Derbyshire pigs of lead were stamped LVT or LVTVD, and have turned up as far afield as Sussex.

Following their normal practice the Romans built durable roads as straight as the country allowed. The road we know as the A515 runs on the Roman line from Buxton south-eastwards. It can be traced past Street House (significant name) to the neighbourhood of Pike Hall, and on again over Minninglow Hill, which carries a group of tumuli. Its line becomes indistinct, but it went on to Derby. Another Roman route, which survives (under the name of Batham Gate), led from Buxton to Navio on the River Noe, a mile from Hope. There it met another road going north-west over the ridge linking Kinder Scout with Win Hill, then up the Woodlands valley, over Doctor's Gate and down to Glossop. No Roman villa, I believe, has been found in the Peak, which suggests that there was no substantial civilian Roman settlement here, only lines of communication. Local labour could have mined the lead with Roman supervision.

Little trace remains of whatever sort of society followed the Roman evacuation. But evidently the Angles or Anglo-Saxons filtered in; a Christian culture is indicated by crosses datable to the eighth century. Under the Normans, the Peak was a Royal Forest, dedicated to breeding and hunting deer, and governed from Peveril Castle at Castleton. It remained modestly busy, if something of a backwater, for the next seven or eight centuries. Many of today's villages are recorded in the Domesday Book; villages, and some single farms, have kept their names recognisably ever since. In the eighteenth century, Arkwright's mills at Cromford gave it a share in the Industrial Revolution; there is still a modest textile industry in the Wye and Derwent valleys and lead mining was a major industry 200 years ago.

Turning now from the Peak itself, the activities of the Peak Park Planning Board are worth studying. What does the Board actually do? Its work has two sides. With one hand, it does for the National Park what a county council's planning committee does for its county. Working under the Town and Country Planning Acts, it exercises control to ensure that the wrong sorts of development do not take place in the National Park. With its other hand, it undertakes various forms of 'positive action', intended to promote public enjoyment of the National Park. The most important of these, perhaps, is to negotiate agreements for access to fine country (like the upper parts of Kinder Scout and Bleaklow). Another sort of positive action is to provide hostels (in Longdendale, for instance, and at Hagg Farm in the Ashop valley) and carefully sited car parks for the innumerable visitors who come to the National Park on wheels. Another is to provide information in various forms, both by publications and at information centres (at Bakewell in the old Market Hall, at Edale, at Buxton, at Castleton and by the use of a mobile van at various places as required).

The planting and maintenance of trees is another field of positive action much used by the Peak Board, sometimes to enhance or maintain natural beauty, sometimes to mitigate the impact of eyesores or of concessions which have been made to social or economic necessity such as houses or quarries in what would otherwise be conspicuous positions; and it manages

for amenity woods which other owners might have to cut and sell. For this work, the board has its own tree nursery and works department.

The Longdendale youth hostel is of particular value, as it fills in a gap in the chain of hostels serving the Pennine Way. It was created by converting and unifying a small row of empty cottages: the board acquired these, adapted them, and handed over the unified building to the Youth Hostels Association to manage.

The most remarkable of all the Peak Board's ventures has been the opening up to public access of many miles of hill country which for years had been strictly preserved for the breeding and shooting of grouse—particularly Kinder Scout and Bleaklow, the two highest hills in the Peak. Here between the wars there had been intermittent trouble between trespassing walkers and gamekeepers, and one notorious 'mass trespass' deliberately organised as a demonstration, which led to something like a pitched battle. The landowners were concerned to ensure that neither the breeding and nesting of grouse nor their eventual shooting should be adversely affected by walkers wandering over the moors, perhaps seriously affecting their sporting value, or starting moor fires by ill-judged camping or picnicking, or carelessly breaking down walls; and they saw no way of doing this but to keep all walkers off the moors. After World War II this disagreement looked like escalating.

It was resolved by a remarkable series of agreements made between the Peak Board and the several owners, whereby access to great areas of moorland was conceded, on the condition that the board and the ramblers' clubs together undertook to enforce a certain discipline of consideration and good sense on the ramblers. Walkers were now able to walk over the high moors (except at specified times, for example when a shoot had been arranged), and

Hikers sitting on the rocky summit of Thorpe Cloud, a hill that towers 900ft above the surrounding countryside, have an almost aerial view of the land around Dovedale. Snug in the gentle contours of the White Peak, farms and villages seem unobtrusive natural phenomena

the Peak Board through its access committee recruited parties of wardens, who saw to it that those who came to walk obeyed sensible rules and restrictions.

The wardens have become a great institution in the Peak. The board has now half-a-dozen staff wardens on its pay-roll, and they find all sorts of ways of, to quote a recent annual report of the board, 'helping and advising visitors to the National Park while protecting the interests of the owners of this scenery'. They are often concerned, for instance, with the relations between farmers and visitors. But their most important purpose remains to see that the agreements for access to the moors work smoothly. On the days agreed for shooting, the wardens, no longer the gamekeepers, post themselves at the main points of entry onto the moors, and direct walkers to the stretches where there is no shooting. In an average season, it has been calculated, there have been about 1,000 attendances by volunteer wardens, over and

Minibuses, one of the Peak Board's answers to holiday traffic problems, bring their passengers up from car parks. At peak times they are the only vehicles allowed in the Goyt Valley which was once choked by visitors' cars

above what is done by the board's staff wardens. At a recent count, there were about 75 square miles covered by access agreements in the Peak.

Besides their duties in respect of access land, the wardens have considerable responsibility in the field of mountain rescue, either in searching for strayed walkers reported missing (perhaps in mist, or after falling and breaking a leg) or in bringing them down when located. They are also sometimes called on to help in putting out moor fires; a year or two ago, wardens took part in extinguishing seventeen moor fires in about seven weeks of high summer. For people wishing to serve as volunteer wardens, weekend training courses are run three or four times a year.

The wardens have recently found a new field of action (very different from Kinder Scout) on the Tissington Trail. This has turned out to be one of the happiest manifestations of positive action. The old railway line from Buxton over the limestone plateau, past Hartington and on to Ashbourne, had long outlived its usefulness (or at least its viability). And what looks more desolate than a disused railway line? In 1969, the Peak Board took over $11\frac{1}{2}$ miles of it, and turned them into a walking and riding route.

This handsome stretch of country had hitherto had no very satisfactory route for the visitor on foot, or on horseback. With the help of volunteer workers, the board cleared the old track of the stones on which the railway lines had rested, established a grass surface good for human or equine feet, equipped the trail with car parks, camp sites and picnic areas and sign-posted long and short excursions from the Trail to adjacent places of special beauty or interest. The whole job took eight years. But there have already been further developments. The Trail has been lengthened at the northern end to reach Parsley Hay, now its highest point. More than that, the board has also acquired $10\frac{1}{2}$ miles of the connecting line from Dow Low, running south-west to Daisy Bank, near Minninglow Hill, and so added the High Peak Trail to the Tissington Trail. An odd thing about the Tissington Trail is that it soon became wildly popular for spon-sored walks, so popular that sponsors had to be rationed.

Another singular enterprise launched in the Peak, promoted and in its experimental stage financed by the Countryside Commission, is the Goyt Valley experiment. This has now passed out of its experimental phase and has become part of the working routine. The problem here was to safeguard an attractive and popular place of resort from being ruined by its own popularity and by the multitude of cars which it attracted in fine weekends.

The upper part of the River Goyt runs through an attractive deep-cut valley from its source on the moors a few miles west of Buxton. It then fills a reservoir, which has apparently done nothing to spoil its attractions, for Goyt's Bridge (at the point of entry) began to attract so many cars on fine weekends as to create serious traffic jams, both at the bridge itself and on the modest lanes which lead down to it on three sides. The charm of the place was destroyed, and pleasure gave way to exasperation.

The solution was a radical one. It involved barring all visiting cars from the waterhead on Sundays, Saturdays and Bank Holidays. A 'motorless zone' was defined, into which cars could not pass: the cars were parked at that point, and their occupants proceeded either on their feet or on coaches provided for the pur-pose. The experiment was well received: a poll of visitors showed about 90 per cent in favour. There may well be a good many other popular places which might benefit by a similar arrange-ment.

Mention must be made of two of the Peak Board's latest adventures: the North Lees Estate and Lose Hill Hall, both of them designed to promote a better understanding of national parks, their context and problems, their possi-bilities and their philosophy.

The North Lees Estate (of 1,265 acres, near Hathersage) came on the market. The Peak Board bought it. The object of this acquisition is designed, as a note in the Board's annual report says, 'to integrate the demands of agriculture, landscape conservation and recreation in a posi-tive way, setting out the framework within which priorities on individual projects will be made'. North Lees may well become a sort of national park laboratory in which various ex-periments which cannot well be mounted on other people's premises, will be tried out.

At Lose Hill Hall, near Castleton, the first national park residential study centre in Britain was formally declared open in November 1972 by Princess Anne. The hall is a Victorian man-sion standing in pleasant parkland, which has been adapted to provide good accommodation for up to sixty people. There is a programme of short courses, varying from three to nine days, on subjects all linked in one way or another with the Peak or with national park problems and practices; it is widely based and includes weeks for anyone over the age of eight and whole families.

Lose Hill Hall is only six or seven miles from the North Lees Estate, and one may hope that some of the courses at the hall will be in touch with the laboratory at North Lees. This may be the beginning of a new and fruitful chapter in the history of national parks in Britain.

Chapter 7

LAKE DISTRICT

C. H. D. Acland

AREA: *866 square miles (224,285ha)*
ALTITUDE: *0 – 3,206ft (0 – 977m)*
　　　　Scafell Pikes 3,206ft (977m)
　　　　Helvellyn 3,116ft (950m)
　　　　Skiddaw 3,054ft (931m)
　　　　Great Gable 2,949ft (899m)
　　　　Pillar 2,927ft (892m)
ADMINISTRATION: *The Lake District National Park Planning Board, a special planning board, has 27 members. 18 are appointed by the Cumbria County Council; 14 represent the County Council and 1 each the District Councils of Allerdale, Eden, South Lakeland, and Copeland. 9 members are appointed by the Secretary of State for the Environment.*
POPULATION: *46,700. Windermere, 8,063; Keswick, 5,169; Ambleside, 2,562; Grasmere, 1,029.*
COMMUNICATIONS: *The only rail service giving access to the park interior is a fairly frequent shuttle service linking Windermere Station to the main north-south electrified line at Oxenholme. There is no service on Sundays.*

By road Kendal to Windermere is 9 miles; Carnforth – Newby Bridge 22 miles; Penrith – Patterdale 15 miles; Carlisle – Keswick 30 miles.

Buses into the park are good, especially from Lancashire, but also from the north and east. There are scheduled bus services up most of the major valleys. The use of minibuses over some of the high passes and smaller roads is developing.

Steamers and motor launches run scheduled services on Windermere, Derwentwater and Ullswater.

VIEWPOINTS *with or near car parks:*
Aira Green (NY 400200)
Derwentwater (NY 270197)
The Tarns (SD 329996)
Whinlatter (NY 224245)
White Moss (NY 345065)
Windermere (SD 403986)
NATIONAL PARK INFORMATION CENTRES:
Ambleside. The Old Courthouse, Church Street; tel Ambleside 3084 (NY 375045)
Ambleside. Waterhead Car Park (mobile) (NY 377033)
Bowness. Bowness Bay, Glebe Road; tel Windermere 2895 (NY 403970)
Hawkshead. Main Car Park (mobile) (NY 354981)
Keswick. The Moot Hall, Market Square; tel Keswick 72803 (NY 266234)
NATIONAL PARK CENTRE, Brockhole, Windermere; *tel Windermere 2231 (NY 389010)*
OTHER VISITOR CENTRES AND MUSEUMS:
Coniston. Ruskin Museum (SD 302977)
Grizedale. Forestry Commission Visitor and Wildlife Centre (SD 335944)
Hawkshead. Courthouse Folk Museum (SD 349987)
Kendal. Abbot Hall Art Gallery and Folk Museum (SD 516922)
Keswick. FitzPark Museum (NY 269237)
NATIONAL PARK INFORMATION OFFICER, *Bank House, High Street, Windermere, Cumbria LA23 1AF*

In the local dialect the word 'spot' is universally used instead of the word 'place'. A shepherd whose tup had won second prize might say that it 'sud 'a' had f'st spot' or that next year he'd show another 'in spot of it'. To describe the Lake District as a spot is correct whether one gives the word its local or its more general meaning. It is very small. It has sometimes been defined as lying within a fifteen-mile radius of the Langdale Pikes or of Dunmail Raise, that pile of stones beside the summit of the main road from Grasmere to Keswick where the body of Gaelic King Dunmail was said to lie until it was discovered that he died in Rome in AD 975. The National Park is rather larger than such a circle. It would need a twenty-mile radius to embrace it, and this would include also the towns of Whitehaven, Cockermouth, Penrith, Kendal and Ulverston which, probably for convenience of administration, have been omitted from it. It is still true that whatever definition is used the Lake District is a mere spot of precious soil in the not-so-very-large island of Great Britain.

It would be instructive for us to look firstly at the geology of the district. The great mass of Skiddaw in the north is about 500 million years old. Although these slates are hard the northern hills are smoothed and rounded by reason of their great antiquity. Next in age is the central core of volcanic rocks. They are equally hard but not smoothed or rounded. They give us the dramatic silhouette of the Langdale Pikes and the climbing faces of Great Gable. Stretching across the south of the district and embracing Coniston Water and Windermere are Silurian rocks, both softer and younger, giving rise to a tamer landscape. At some time this great dome sank into the sea and was covered with layers, first of Carboniferous Limestone, then of Coal Measures and lastly of Red Sandstone. After it rose again these layers became slowly eroded from the central fells until today they occur only round the perimeter, the limestone notably at Kendal Fell, the coal at Whitehaven and the sandstone at Penrith and St Bees. The other geological incident of uncertain date is the granite, intruded in a liquid state and now out-cropping at Shap and in Eskdale.

By comparison with the age of the rocks the effect of the climate is recent, even though the last main Ice Age ended some 15,000 years ago. At one time the highest fells were covered with ice, as witness the scars left by ice-borne boulders etched in the solid rock on the summit of Bow-fell. But it was in the dales that the ice left its major mark on our scenery. It was the glaciers, flowing outwards from the centre which carved the main U-shaped valleys such as Langdale and Borrowdale. These have flat floors, now occupied by the characteristic hay meadows, and steep sides with waterfalls spouting from hanging valleys high on their flanks. Confusingly at least three of these white cascades have earned for themselves the name of Sour Milk Gill. It was the glaciers which gouged out the depressions which now contain the lakes, some of them such as Windermere and Wastwater going well below sea-level, and it was the moraines deposited as the ice rivers retreated which helped to impound the lakes themselves.

The more recent climate has earned for the Lake District a sadly exaggerated reputation. Admittedly the rainfall can be measured in feet rather than inches but the actual hours of rainfall in a year are not significantly more than in many other places. Rare is the day which is wholly wet.

Apart from the lakes and waterfalls which would be nothing without the rain, its effect on our luxuriant tree growth plays a dominant part in the scenery. Nowhere, except on the high tops and a few valley heads, is the landscape not dependent on trees. Who could imagine Borrowdale without its woods? Who

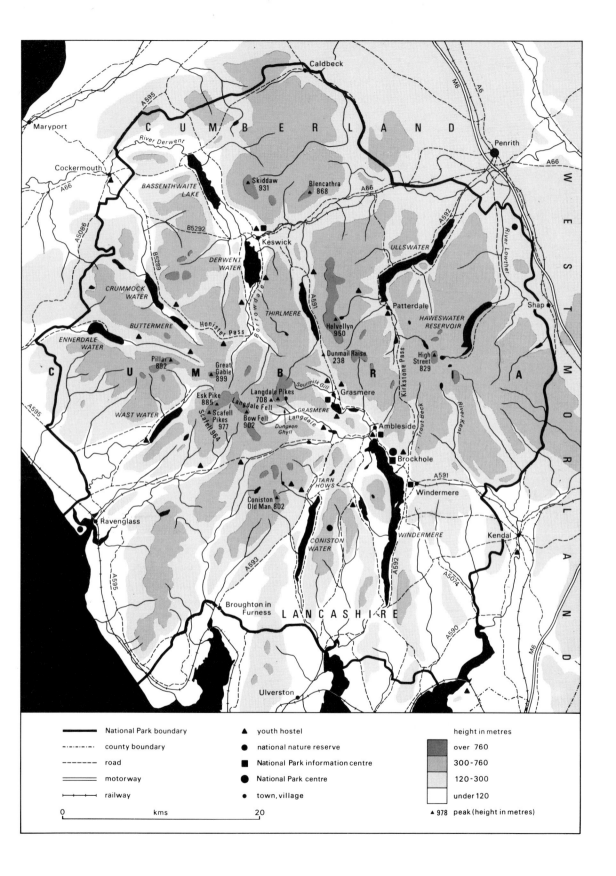

CUMBERLAND

WESTMORLAND

LANCASHIRE

CUMBRIA

Maryport

Cockermouth

A66

A5086

A595

River Derwent

A595

Caldbeck

M6

A6

Penrith

A66

B5292

Skiddaw
931

Blencathra
868

A66

River Lowther

Keswick

BASSENTHWAITE
LAKE

DERWENT
WATER

B5289

CRUMMOCK
WATER

THIRLMERE

Borrowdale

ULLSWATER

A592

Shap

River Lowther

BUTTERMERE

Honister Pass

A591

Patterdale

HAWESWATER
RESERVOIR

ENNERDALE
WATER

Pillar
892

Great
Gable
899

Helvellyn
950

Dunmail Raise
238

High
Street
829

Kirkstone Pass

C

U

M

B

R

I

A

Esk Pike
885

Langdale Pikes
708

Sourmilk Gill

Grasmere

River Kent

WAST WATER

Scafell
Pikes
977

Langdale Fell

GRASMERE

Bow Fell
902

Langdale

Scafell 964

Dungeon
Ghyll

Ambleside

Trout Beck

Brockhole

A591

TARN
HOWS

Windermere

Coniston
Old Man 802

A593

CONISTON
WATER

WINDERMERE

Kendal

A592

A5074

Ravenglass

Broughton in
Furness

A595

LANCASHIRE

A590

M6

Ulverston

0   kms   20

National Park boundary

county boundary

road

motorway

railway

▲ youth hostel

● national nature reserve

■ National Park information centre

⬤ National Park centre

• town, village

height in metres

over 760

300-760

120-300

under 120

▲ 978   peak (height in metres)

could recognise Tarn Hows shorn of its fringing trees, even though many of them are conifers planted in the last century, rather than primeval oaks? The ready and often natural regeneration of woods and trees relies much on the abundant rainfall.

The first traces of man's occupation are found on the coastal plain where Middle and Late Stone Age settlements appear to overlap. In the heart of the high fells stone axe factories have been discovered in many places, almost wherever the fine-grained stone suitable for this skilled craft exists. (Stone Age man was a competent geologist.) The axes, which were roughed out in the factories and finished on the coast where the sandstone was available for polishing, were exported widely over Britain. The real significance of the axe is that it enabled man for the first time to clear the forest and scrub which had colonised the district since the ice departed. Thus started man's modification of 'natural beauty' which has continued ever since. Several stone circles, notably at Keswick, Shap and Swinside near Millom, are of the Bronze Age but otherwise knowledge of this period, and of the Iron Age which preceded the Roman invasion, is largely lacking.

The Romans, coming as conquerors rather than settlers, drove their roads north to Carlisle and the Wall soon after AD 70, and branched west by High Street, Wrynose and Hardknott, where the most impressive fort can be seen, to Ravenglass, their never-used 'invasion port' for Ireland. By about AD 383 they ceased to have any real presence in the Lake District and the Celtic natives reverted to the illiteracy of the Dark Ages. How little this great exploit marked the Lakes!

This cannot be said of the next invaders, the Angles and the Vikings from Scandinavia. Coming partly across country, and partly round the north of Scotland, they occupied all the valleys with their grazing sheep, establishing the existing pattern of farms and giving us the place-names which we know today. Dale, gill, beck, tarn and force (a waterfall) are all Norse words, but the most significant is *thwaite*. It means a clearing in a wood. Subsequently the district was parcelled out amongst the Norman barons who gave large parts of it to the monasteries such as Furness, Shap, Cartmel and even Fountains. The monks and other landowners continued clearing the woods for sheep grazing to serve the wool trade. The flat valley floors began to be drained for agriculture.

They cut the primeval woods also to make charcoal for smelting. Iron was worked mainly in Furness, copper in Borrowdale and at Coniston, lead at Glenridding and wad or black lead was mined at Seathwaite, giving rise to Keswick's still-thriving pencil industry. Today, of course, we try to keep national parks free of such mineral workings! The slate quarries were not worked on a big scale until the eighteenth century but they are still worked today, though now they produce sawn slabs for the cladding of buildings, rather than roofing slates. Charcoal was needed, not only for smelting but for making gunpowder, an industry which thrived until after World War I. The scars from these industries, including the pitsteads or platforms where the charcoal burner made his smouldering fires, can still be seen where the noise of mining has long ceased, and where the wooded fellsides are now bare of trees.

Man's effect upon the woodlands was not wholly destructive. Greenwich Hospital became the owners of the east shore of Derwentwater when the earl of that name lost his estates and his head after the '45 rebellion. They planted

---

The Lake District has always been famed for its beauty and this view of Grasmere, the area particularly favoured by Wordsworth and Coleridge, captures a unique blend of calm water and impressive hillside

extensively after their fellings. John Christian Curwen is said to have planted a million trees beside Windermere in 1787. The Marshall family came from Yorkshire in the early nineteenth century and bought estates beside several of the lakes, investing part of their wool fortune in trees whose grand maturity is enjoyed to this day.

Agricultural improvement came later than it did in the rest of England. The manorial system with its common fields never fully developed. As a result there were few great landed estates; there were no 'villeins'; the farmers were yeomen, known as 'statesmen' who owned the land they farmed. The social division between squire, farmer and labourer has never existed in the Lakes. The visitor will do well to remember that the shepherd who thinks (and smells) of sheep still regards the land as his own heritage.

Buildings, too, developed late. Although one or two bigger houses, notably the picturesque Coniston Hall, and chapels such as Wasdale Head, were built in the sixteenth century and although several grammar schools, including Hawkshead, were founded shortly after the Reformation, it was not until the mid-seventeenth century that the clay or wooden and thatched dwellings gave place to stone. At first they were primitive: the doorway entered the kitchen, the parlour being to one side; behind the parlour was the dairy or store and behind the kitchen the stairs (unroofed at first), led to the sleeping loft above. This pattern can still often be seen, not least the dairy with its slate slabs on which bacon has been salted for generations.

Since stone is stone and slate is slate it is not always easy to tell the old from the new. There are two rough guides. Old slates were thick and rough; new ones are thin and smooth. Reroofing of an old building may efface this clue to its age, so look next at the quoins or corner stones. Lay your hand flat on the table and cover the fingers with the flat fingers of the other hand; this was the old way of building a quoin. Now lay your hand on edge and lay the little finger of the other hand on the forefinger of the first, thus gaining maximum height for the least amount of 'stone'. Such a quoin is more recent.

Characteristically, the houses were whitened with lime every year until two or three hundred coats of lime have produced almost the effect of plaster. This lime, and the plaster on the inside of the walls, keeps out the wind. But the barns and other farm buildings, built entirely without mortar, were left bare. As a result of the wind that blows through the walls cattle with tuberculosis and fires from heated hay are almost unknown.

The stone walls round the fields came later still. Although some fields, notably the irregular enclosures at Wasdale Head, are very ancient, most of the walls date from the late eighteenth or early nineteenth centuries. On the valley floors the field pattern is often rectangular but on the sides of the valleys larger irregular pieces have been taken in from the common or allotted to a particular man at the time of the enclosure awards, hence the two names 'intak's' and 'allotments' which describe these sloping areas. The labour of walling them must have been immense but one should remember that until the wall was up the owner could keep neither his own sheep in, nor his neighbour's out. To wall was to own.

A wall is much narrower at the top than at the base. It consists of two fences with a well filled core between them. 'Through' stones, often seen as a projecting line half way up a wall (or as lines across the gable end of a barn), bind the two faces together. The top stones, called cams, usually project more to one side of a wall than to the other. The place where the cams change sides often marks the place where one farmer's responsibility for repairs gives way to another's. 'Cams against your neighbour', as they say. Although most lakeland farmers are still good stone-wallers, it is hard work and takes time to put up a gap thrown down in a couple of seconds by a walker too thoughtless or idle to keep to a path or find a stile.

The main Kendal to Carlisle road passed by the Lake District, as did many other important affairs of state. Communications remained primitive. Dorothy Wordsworth rode pillion behind William from Grasmere to Keswick where now the largest road of the district flies over Dunmail Raise. Pack horses were the main transport until the late eighteenth century. Paradoxically their early routes traversed country where now there is no road at all. Perhaps a score of the old pack bridges, narrow and low-sided to allow a bulky load to pass, can still be identified in such valley heads as Wasdale, Eskdale and Borrowdale, and in Easedale there still stands 'Willie Goodwaller Bridge' (may he lie easy in his grave). The adventurous visitors of the nineteenth century were by no means the first to cross the high passes of Sty Head, Stake or Ore Gap.

Visitors began to come to the Lakes in the second half of the eighteenth century. Gray, in 1769, was one of the first to write of his tour, and although we should now consider him un-adventurous (he dared not penetrate Borrowdale beyond Grange) he writes of the beauty of the scenery in terms which we can only envy. 'Not a single red tile, no gentleman's glaring house or garden walls, break in upon the repose' of Grasmere. West wrote the first guide to the Lakes while Wordsworth was still a boy at Hawkshead Grammar School. The tourist trade was beginning to develop.

The railway reached Windermere in 1847 and Coniston and Keswick by 1865. Roads were improved and extended so that even before the invention of the car it was possible to drive up all the valleys and over all the passes which now have motor roads. Manchester opened their Thirlmere reservoir in 1894 and Haweswater in 1940. The car penetrated at about the time of World War I. The Forestry Commission was set up just afterwards with the avowed object of growing quick conifer crops to provide the sort of timber needed for trench warfare. By an arrangement made with the Council for the Preservation of Rural England in 1936 they agreed not to acquire land for planting in the heart of the district, but Coniston, Ennerdale, Skiddaw and the Duddon were heavily planted (so was Thirlmere, by Manchester Corporation). Wealthy industrialists from Lancashire's prosperous cotton towns bought up sites for their big houses, especially along the east shore of Windermere. The south-west shore of Ullswater was lotted up in building plots.

This rapid development did not go unchallenged. Wordsworth opposed the railway to Windermere and the level road from Rydal to Grasmere which replaced the steep track over Whitemoss Common. The Commons, Open Spaces and Footpaths Preservation Society was set up in 1865 and the Lake District Defence Society—forerunner of the Friends of the Lake District—in 1883. In 1895 the National Trust came into being. One of its founders was Canon Rawnsley, Vicar of Crosthwaite near Keswick, and a great protector of the Lakes.

The National Trust has had a major influence on the Lakes. It is easy to forget that during the first half of its life there was no planning law to prevent even the most outrageous development. Moreover in those early days private land was private. The Trust launched appeals and bought threatened lake shores, often at full building value. In every case it gave free public access on foot to these acquisitions, notably beside Derwentwater and Ullswater and near Bowness and Ambleside. Since the late 1920s when George Trevelyan, the historian, spent most of his patrimony to buy the head of Great Langdale for the Trust, it has become the biggest landowner in the district. It now owns about one-fifth of the area of the park. Although its main object continues to be preservation—of landscape, woods and traditional buildings, not to mention traditional sheep farming—its interest in access and the people has made it by far the greatest provider of those facilities—car parks, camp sites, adventure huts, etc—without which the public either cannot enjoy the scenery or will actually spoil what there is.

The scenery and atmosphere of the fells owes much to the mountain sheep. The origins of the indigenous Herdwick breed are unknown. Legends about the Spanish Armada or the Vikings are not substantiated by any related breed in Spain, Scandinavia or even Iceland. Its wool is coarse and full of hair but it makes hard-wearing tweed. Because the lambs are mainly born black and grow paler each year as they mature, it is possible to produce a patterned (but undyed) tweed by selecting wools of different ages. Although the Herdwick has been replaced to some extent by the Swaledale which produces more valuable wool it remains the toughest and most reliable breed for the fells. Its characteristics include its instinct to stay on its own piece of fell, the place where it was heafed or hefted when its mother took it as a lamb to her own heaf. This is why so much of the fell land does not need to be fenced. It has also a remarkable power of foretelling snowfalls and taking avoiding action by dropping to lower ground. If it is overblown it can survive for many weeks beneath a drift, emerging, poor thing, quite naked but alive, having eaten all its own wool.

Today the fell sheep is the architect of the scenery of the Lakes. Without it the uneaten grass would become matted and unpleasant to walk on, the fells would revert to scrub and

the open view would be obscured. The sheep is the cheapest and best park keeper there has ever been. But do not make the mistake of thinking that the shepherd, too, is a park keeper. Without him, and without the prosperity of fell farming upon which he must depend, it is true that the whole aspect of the National Park would change. But he himself is a hard-working farmer. For three weeks at lambing time he works a seventeen-hour day. He does this for his sheep, and because his living depends on it, not for the visitors who enjoy the sheep-cropped fells.

In its pursuit of cheap food industrial Britain has continuously subsidised the end product of its agriculture, paying out to ensure that milk, meat, bread and potatoes can be bought reasonably by the city dwellers. The rugged parts of Cumbria cannot produce their sheep as an end product, the farmer cannot fatten his lambs on the fells. He must sell them as store sheep to the lowlander who has better pastures, pastures which come into growth earlier in the spring, and it is the lowlander who fattens them and sells them to the butcher who turns them into mutton. It is the lowlander who reaps the reward and does not necessarily pass on an adequate share of it to the breeder.

To redress this fault, and to ensure that there are enough store sheep for our mutton requirements, subsidies for hill sheep have been given directly to the hill farmer. Unless these are adequate (and at the time of writing they are scarcely so), the fell farmer will go out of business—not immediately, for, like his sheep, he is heafed on his fell—but within the foreseeable future there could be no farms in the valleys, no sheep on the fells. It could be that the valley floors would be ranched by summer cattle belonging to lowland farmers. The walls would go down, each farmstead would become a hostel or cafeteria. In the absence of sheep the only economic use of the fell sides, the only employment for the rural population, would be

Sheep have always played an important part in the fellside way of
life and despite the gross intrusion of visitors at peak holiday times,
farming on the hills is a lonely occupation

forestry—not the small mixed woodlands so
pleasant in the landscape and so useful for access,
but massed planting of Sitka spruce. God grant
this may never happen.

The fell farmer's life is not all hard graft. In
the winter he takes part in fox hunting which is
done on foot with the prime object of reducing
the number of foxes which he has good reason
to regard as vermin. In the summer there are
village sports and shows. These vary widely; at
Grasmere, which has become mainly a tourist
attraction, there is wrestling in the traditional

Cumberland style and there is also the incredible
guide's race (still usually won by a farmer's
son) which involves leaping up and down 800ft
of steep fellside in the space of 12 minutes; at
Wasdale Head, very late in the season, the
judging and discussion of sheep is briefly inter-
rupted by the hound trails. These trails are races
run by dogs which appear to be half foxhound
and half greyhound, following the line of a drag,
laid with aniseed and paraffin. The farmer comes
into his own at the sheepdog trials. One after
another through the whole day, each farmer,

controlling his dog by whistled signals, makes it drive three sheep round a set course and then confine them in a pen. This is done against the clock; the suspense as the seconds tick by and the stubborn sheep refuse to be penned, can be unbearable.

The natural history of the Lake District while not spectacular is always interesting and worth hunting for. Like the topography it is derived from the ancient rocks, most of which are acid in nature, giving rise to soils and waters less rich than those of limestone origin, and supporting a less varied wildlife. The high fells support an alpine-arctic flora and in some high places there are natural rock gardens which are worth the necessary hunt and scramble. Here, one may find the northern bedstraw, the alpine lady's mantle and mountain form of saxifrage and the club mosses and parsley fern. On the lower ground there are interesting bogs, called locally 'mosses'. Amongst insects the small mountain ringlet butterfly has its only English colonies high on the fells, and the netted carpet moth, which requires as its food plant the yellow balsam which grows well beside Windermere, is also unique. The charming pied-flycatcher is a local bird, arriving regularly during the last four days in April to build its nest in holes in trees, or in nesting boxes. The redbreasted merganser, a fish-eating duck, has established itself on Windermere during the last twenty years and the golden eagle has, for the first time this century, successfully reared its young.

In the woods, still largely oak, though not always primeval, there are interesting and rare mosses and other lower plants, particularly on north-facing slopes which never dry out. The pine marten amongst mammals is rare, but the squirrels of the Lake District are plentiful and red—not grey. There are red deer too in the woods between Windermere and Coniston Water and on the open fells east of Ullswater. The char, a fish related to the trout and salmon,

lives in a few of the deeper lakes. It appears to be a left-over from the Ice Age, being known also from Scandinavia.

The Nature Conservancy with its research station at Grange-over-Sands has established several nature reserves within the park, of which the main interests are woodland and wet lands. Most of the reserves of the Lake District Naturalists' Trust are outside the park, but at Whitbarrow Scar they have an interesting limestone plateau. The Forestry Commission has a wildlife centre at Grisedale where the emphasis is on deer, including high seats for watching them.

It is easier to enumerate the factors, both natural and man-made, which have affected the scenery of the Lakes, than to describe the scenery itself and to say just why its preservation and enjoyment are so important. The mountains of Switzerland are much higher, with snow to boot. The Highlands of Scotland are far more extensive, and in these days of rapid travel, almost as accessible. What is it that distinguishes our 'spot'? Why does it occupy such a warm place in the hearts and memories of so many of its visitors?

Perhaps the scale of the scenery is its most particular attribute. Although man has overcome his eighteenth-century horror of the beetling cliff and his terror of the dreadful chasm, and although the majority of visitors come to the country with the object of 'getting away from it all', does not man still like to feel in touch with humanity? Does he find true recreation when he is overawed by nature, made to feel puny and insignificant? In the Lake District the scale of man's activities is just right. He has come to terms with nature rather than taming it. The farmer and his sheep use the whole of the country, but have not imposed themselves on it; they have neither oppressed it nor possessed it. The farmstead on the valley floor bears a kindly

Another side of the Lake District which is becoming all too familiar. Heavy vehicles – are they a necessary evil or should firmer steps be taken to keep them outside the national park?

relationship with the fells above it. The fells often appear higher than they really are, but still not so high as to be unattainable. The youthful, in a couple of hours, and the middle-aged within a day can reach any of the tops, and from the tops can look down on to a ribbon of valley, or several ribbons of several valleys, in which the pattern of fields is the reminder that one is not in complete wilderness.

Nor is solitude lacking for those who seek it. Go to Tarn Hows on a Sunday afternoon in summer, climb to the top of Great Gable and there will be other folk about. But come in the winter or the evening, wander from the beaten track—only 200yd to the left or to the right—you are alone!

There are, however, some threats to the park and, to quote the Act, 'to preserving and enhancing its natural beauty ... and promoting its enjoyment by the public'. First amongst these in everyone's mind is traffic and the consequent demand for wider roads which would be quite out of scale with the country. It will be neces-

sary to introduce schemes for traffic management, and most important of all, to implement the power already given by Act of Parliament to regulate and prohibit certain kinds of traffic, particularly the over-large coach or the heavy tanker.

The over-commercialisation of the tourist trade is also to be feared. So long as the trade recognises that it serves the visitor it is wholly desirable and its development entirely proper. The boat for hire on the lake, the bus to put you down at the right point to start your expedition, the pint at the pub when you complete a long walk, the farmhouse tea or accommodation, the hostel, the holiday centre, the lodging house and the hotel, even the caravan site for touring vans —these are right and necessary if the people are to enjoy the Lakes as they should be enjoyed. And it is absolutely right that those who provide these services should make a fair living. What is to be deplored is the bingo hall, the gimmick, the plastic bunting to call attention to a petrol station. It is delightful to see Windermere or Ullswater from the steamers which ply on these two large lakes, but nothing can be more out of place than the blaring of music from their loud-speakers, audible not only to the passengers, but to everyone within a range of two, three or even more miles. It is no fun fishing the evening rise along the shore, watching roe deer in the woods or listening to the conversation of a family of longtailed tits to the accompaniment of the sound of the latest pop tunes.

There are also some sports or pastimes which naturally accord with the district and others which are less suitable. Broadly speaking those which depend on the intrinsic qualities of the district are acceptable. Obviously walking is pre-eminent amongst these, nor can one climb Middlefell Buttress except at the head of Great Langdale. The whole enjoyment of scenery—sketching, photography, just sitting on the grass or going for a drive in the car, perhaps even sitting in it and reading the paper—owes its pleasure to the surrounding country. But there are some sports which derive little from the intrinsic beauty of the Lakes, for example motor rallies by night, and some which may even conflict with the enjoyment of others. It is difficult to believe that water-skiing, practised by only a few scores, should be allowed to create noise and turmoil over such a large proportion of several lakes. It is to be hoped that the park authority will soon exercise its power under the Countryside Act of 1968 to solve this conflict of interests.

Another problem which causes deep antagonism between residents and visitors is the demand for second homes. It is not unnatural that increasing prosperity and leisure amongst those who live and work in the industrial areas to the south and east should give rise to the desire to have a cottage in the Lake District. But it is frustrating in the extreme when the local worker, in the woods, the quarries or in the tourist trade, is unable to find anywhere to live. Young people who cannot find, or afford, houses tend to move away. Some of the wealthy owners of second homes complain that nowadays it is quite impossible to find anyone to do their gardens!

In several respects the work of the Lake District Planning Board has differed from that of authorities in charge of other parks. Like the Peak Planning Board, the Lakes Board is an independent authority. This gives it a healthy measure of independence, still coupled with a sensitivity towards local needs, a sensitivity stemming from the fact that two-thirds of its members are county council appointments and the other third, who are appointed by the Secretary of State for the Environment, have almost always been drawn from people who live and work within the boundaries of the park. But whereas the Peak has always employed its own planning staff, the Lakes 'borrowed' from the three county councils until 1974, since when it, too, has appointed its own staff. Before this change was made the Lakes, for twenty-three years, had lacked the clear leadership which has been outstanding in the Peak District, and there had sometimes been conflicting loyalties when county council development came before the Board.

Because of the pressure from residents and from those who live in surrounding areas the number of applications for planning permission far exceeds those dealt with in any other park, and on the whole success in this direction has been outstanding. Development has mainly been contained within existing communities and although some plans have not been of the highest standard, not a great deal that is really bad has got past the watchful eyes of the Board.

It has always been the tradition among the amiable Lake District farmers to allow the public to walk on their open land, and for this reason, coupled with the absence of grouse and valuable sporting rights, there has been little need to make access agreements. The park wardens, a handful of full-time men and several scores of volunteers, devote themselves to the safety and enjoyment of visitors rather than herding them on to, or away from, access or private land.

The Lakes Board leads the way amongst parks in helping visitors to find out about the countryside, what it has to offer and how to enjoy it. At Brockhole, on the shore of Windermere, is the Lake District National Park Centre where visitors—individually or in parties—can learn about the geology and the history, the wildlife and the human life, the culture and the beauty of the district. Every year this centre is visited by increasing thousands who come to learn how to appreciate rather than spoil the wealth of recreation and beauty that is the Lake District.

Chapter 8

YORKSHIRE DALES

Arthur Raistrick

AREA: *680 square miles (176,113ha)*

ALTITUDE: *393– 2,419ft (120– 737m)*
Whernside 2,419ft (737m)
Ingleborough 2,373ft (723m)
Great Shunner Fell 2,340ft (713m)
Great Whernside 2,310ft (704m)
Pen-y-ghent 2,277ft (694m)

ADMINISTRATION: *The Yorkshire Dales National Park Committee, a separate committee of the North Yorkshire County Council, has 24 members of whom 16 are appointed by the County Council; 12 represent the North Yorkshire County Council, 1 the Cumbria County Council, and 1 each the District Councils of Richmondshire, Craven, and South Lakeland. 8 members are appointed by the Secretary of State for the Environment.*

POPULATION: *20,700. Sedbergh, 2,219; Grassington, 1,131.*

COMMUNICATIONS: *Harrogate is linked to the Intercity rail network, but has no bus service into the park. Skipton and Settle, poorly served by rail from Leeds and Shipley, have bus services into the park. Stations at Kendal and Oxenholme are linked by bus with Sedbergh and Dent in the park. Buses from Darlington on the main line serve Wensleydale.*

By road Richmond to Aysgarth is 19 miles; Harrogate – Grassington 24 miles; Skipton – Grassington 9 miles; Kendal – Sedbergh 11 miles.

Motorists approaching from the south can use the

M1 to Leeds and enter the park via Ilkley. Exits 34 to 38 on the M6 are convenient for the park from the west.

Within the park there are buses serving Wharfedale, Ribblesdale, Malhamdale, Wensleydale, and Swaledale.

VIEWPOINTS *with or near car parking:*
Abbotside (SD 866927)
Bowland Knotts (SD 726607)
Buttertubs (SD 874961)
Dodd Fell (SD 841846)
Fancarl (SE 060630)
Newby Head (SD 780842)

NATIONAL PARK INFORMATION CENTRES:
Aysgarth Falls; tel Aysgarth 424 (SE 012889)
Clapham. Reading Room; tel Clapham 419 (SD 746693)
Malham. The Car Park; tel Airton 363 (SD 900626)

OTHER VISITOR CENTRES, MUSEUMS:
Appletreewick. Folk and Farming Implements Museum (SE 053602)
Bowes. Museum (NY 996136)
Castle Bolton. Museum (SE 034918)
Skipton. Craven Museum (SD 990518)

NATIONAL PARK OFFICER, *Yorkshire Dales National Park Committee, Thornborough Hall, Leyburn, Yorkshire DL8 5AB*

The essence of the Yorkshire Dales National Park is the ever-present contrast of two worlds, each of very pronounced and unmistakable character. There is no area where these merge, you are in one or the other, the connecting links being the hill farmers, shepherds and game-keepers who use and work in the uplands but live in the valleys. On the high fells which occupy the major area of the park, one can walk for miles in solitude meeting only sheep and the occasional shepherd, seeing and hearing curlews and grouse, the occasional merlin or even the solitary buzzard. It is a world of heather, peat haggs, cotton grass or moor grass, of strenuous effort rewarded by unsurpassed views across the Pennine summits and away to the Lake District mountains.

In the dales there are farms and villages with a friendly population, cattle in the fields and common pastures, and a surprising richness of rural scenery. There are fine rivers, waterfalls and crags, and spectacular limestone gorges and hidden valleys. To cross from one dale to another demands a steep climb of many hundreds of feet onto the 'tops', and then a steep descent back into the world of the valleys. The roads, adequate for the market business of the dalesfolk, are few enough, fortunately, to leave areas of wild fells accessible only to the walker, who can secure a full day of solitude if he knows his country. The pressure of the motorist for the upgrading of some of the ancient drove roads and green tracks which cross these 'tops' must be resisted at all costs.

While the principal dales impose an approximate east-west grain on the area, the major watershed is that of the Pennines north to south, dominated by two groups of high fells through which the long distance path of the Pennine Way takes its exhilarating course. In the south-west part, recent generations of visitors have popularised the Three Peaks by organising frequent competitive foot races on a circuit which includes the three summits. The newly christened Three Peaks are Pen-y-ghent (2,277ft), Ingleborough (2,373ft) and Whernside (2,419ft), true peaks which tower above a surrounding

plateau of limestone pavements and are so distinctive in their individual shapes as to be recognised from many distant viewpoints in the park. They form a focal point for which one searches instinctively when looking towards the south or south-west. Actually the Three Peaks are only part of a circle of fells completed on the north by Widdale Fell (2,203ft) and Dodd Fell (2,189ft). The wide area of Ribblehead is enclosed by these five giants, being itself a bowl of moorland with a base level over 1,400ft OD.

From this bowl, with its ring of peaks and moorland ridges which the Park Planning Committee would like to see designated as a 'wilderness area', but which the private forestry interests are desecrating with their ugly blankets of coniferous trees, many rivers run. Here the Ribble has its source and its dale opens out and runs south between Ingleborough and Pen-y-ghent. Chapel-le-Dale, the valley of the Greta, lies between Ingleborough and Whernside. West of Whernside is Kingsdale, short and wild with only two farms, sharing with the Greta the splendid gorges of the Ingleton Glens where spectacular waterfalls and rock gorges crowd on one another in a fantastic round of two miles of thickly wooded 'scenery'. Two rivers run to the west, the Dee through Dentdale and the Clough through Garsdale, both joining the Rawthey near Sedbergh. The northern part of the great bowl is Newby head where Widdale with its river, a large tributary of the Ure, descends to the north. Eastwards the heads of the Wharfe and Skirfare lead into Wharfedale and Littondale. Only the Aire among the southern rivers has no connection with Ribblehead but rises in the fells between Ribble and Wharfe.

Around Ribblehead and the Three Peaks is the limestone land of Craven, a vast area of bare limestone pavements, crags and scars, with caves and potholes almost beyond counting. This is a unique landscape sufficient on its own merit to justify the designation of a national park.

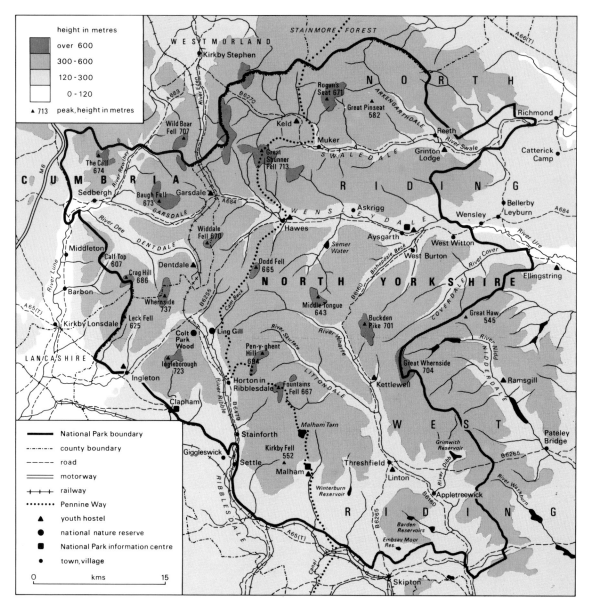

This land has its unexpected patches of high colour which come as something of a surprise—the golden spread of the globe flowers on the approach to Malham Tarn from Langcliffe is a sight not easily forgotten. The blue moor-grass in season can spread a shimmering blue haze over large areas of upland grass, and among the grey scars the grass has a vivid green not matched elsewhere. Everywhere on the limestone fells there is the rich scent of thymes and other aromatic herbage.

The apparent bareness of the limestone pavement is actually an illusion. The grykes, the crevices in the pavement, provide a sheltered habitat for a number of fine plants including the hart's tongue and hard shield ferns, and herb

106

robert. Most of the limestone scars have screes below them on much of which there is a belt of trees, ash, sycamore, hawthorn, hazel and guelder rose being particularly common. The screes also carry a very special flora in parts, and on the face of the limestone cliffs the yew is a common relief to the white of the limestone. On some of the more open screes and limestone pastures the mealy primrose spreads large carpets of colour in spring, while such open woodland as Bastow Wood in Wharfedale and other woods on the valley sides have wide carpets of lily-of-the-valley, bloody cranesbill or rock rose.

The bird population in these woods is rich and varied, as rewarding to the ornithologist as the flora is to the botanist. A bird which is relatively common in the dales' streams is the dipper. Sometimes a heron can be seen quietly fishing in a stream although a sighting on main river banks is perhaps more likely. On the moors, besides the grouse large flocks of golden plover are to be expected and in a few choice spots the raven and the buzzard are still about.

North of Wensleydale the River Swale is the sole major river of another comparable horseshoe of high fells. Starting on the northern watershed of Wensleydale and proceeding clockwise, there is Lovelyseat or Lunnersett (2,213ft), Great Shunner Fell (2,340ft), Hugh Seat (2,251ft), High Seat (2,328ft), High Pike Hill (2,105ft), then north of the pass of Birkdale (1,699ft), at Lamps Moss, we come to the mystery of Nine Standards Rigg (2,170ft) with its erratic collection of high cairns. After the gap of Tan Hill (which has many ancient and unexpected coal mines) we cross to Rogan's Seat (2,203ft) and Water Crag (2,188ft) where the country declines slowly to the south-east. This group of fells encircles the first ten miles of the Swale which, with its tributaries, flows through the area in narrow valleys and impressive gorges. The heather moorlands finally decline to about 1,600ft, and continue at this height for another nine miles or so on each side of Swaledale. They are one of the finest 'solitude' areas in the North.

To give any adequate description of the many dales which penetrate these uplands is far beyond the limits of this chapter. Although there are only seven principal river valleys they all have tributary valleys, some of impressive size, so that more than twenty dales are found in the park. All provide a wealth of fine scenery for exploration. Each dale has a character of its own, different from all the others, and yet retains some essential elements that are common to all; there is thus unity in diversity. Narrow valley bottoms, broadening in their mid-course, hold the meadows of the dairy farms. The enclosed pastures climb the valley sides to the moor wall above which the unenclosed high moors lie. Along the length of each major valley there is a string of villages, not on the riverside but perched on a terrace, sometimes glacial, sometimes the first of the limestone terraces or else the delta of a tributary stream. They are small, usually with populations ranging between less than fifty to two or three hundred, only a very few being larger than this. The only 'towns' are Hawes at the head of Wensleydale, a market town of just over 1,100 and the larger town of Sedbergh, just over 2,000, swelled by the presence of the public school.

The chief glory of the dales is the abundance of fine waterfalls and the numerous splendid limestone features. Both are a result of the geological structure. This part of the Pennines is formed in the Carboniferous series of rocks, massive Great Scar Limestone followed by the Yoredale Series which has many thinner limestones, shales and sandstones. The lower part of the thick series is of the Millstone Grit. Except for the north-west corner the rocks of the park are folded into a flattish dome with a centre near Ribblehead, so that the strata have a gentle outward dip. The west and south sides are cut off abruptly by the big dislocations of the Dent and Craven Faults which are responsible among others for such scenic features as Giggleswick Scars, Malham Cove and some of the exciting gorges of the streams on the east side of the Rawthey valley. The general effect of this structure is that the Great Scar Limestone up to 800ft thick makes a high plateau in the south-west on which the Three Peaks rear their bulk, and then declines to the north-east so that the limestones of Malham and Malham Moor pass into the massive scars of Kilnsey Crag and of Wharfedale. In Wensleydale the limestones are in the valley bottom. The wonderful waterfalls in the river at Aysgarth are over successive beds of this limestone. In Swaledale it forms the scenery around Kisdon, between Muker and Keld, and the high crags of Fremington Edge in Arkengarthdale.

The Yoredale Series is named from the valley of the Ure now better known as Wensleydale, where the many limestones each make a mile-long scar and terrace along the valley side. As a consequence of this every tributary stream has a long succession of waterfalls and gorges as it crosses sandstones and limestones one after another. Waterfalls of every size and description, ranging from those falling 3ft to those falling 80ft, are a particular feature of this national park. The dip takes down the Yoredales as it has done the Great Scar Limestone, so that in the north-east and east the vast heather-covered moorlands of Millstone Grit are predominant, their dark browns and russets relieved only by a sprinkling of cotton-grass blooms until they burst into autumnal glory with the flowering of the heather. In the north-west across the Dent Fault and the Rawthey valley we come across those heralds of the Lake District—the lovely velvety grass-covered slopes of the slate hills of the Howgills. Valleys are steep and narrow and occupied by mountain torrents. Crags are few

and screes are of slate.

Human history has been long and varied during the 12,000 years since the glaciers which covered the area in the Ice Age finally disappeared. The reclothing with trees and grassland was slow and the climate varied, being often cold and wet, so that the earliest settlement by man was only slight. Evidence of the earliest folk is almost confined to the minute flint implements they used, arrow and harpoon points and a few tools of the migrant hunters of the Mesolithic period, about 7000 to 3000 BC. The Neolithic people began some forest clearance but it was not until the Bronze Age, about 1800 BC to a few centuries before the Roman invasion, that, with the exception of the Giant's Graves, Pen-y-ghent, large communal monuments were made. Then stone circles, such as Yockenthwaite, and the large earthwork circles called 'henges' (Castle Dykes and Yarnbury are examples), were erected. The people lived in small circular huts, the foundations of which are to be seen very often although it is not easy to distinguish between those of Bronze Age and those of Romano-British people.

The Iron Age people were part of an invasion from the Continent and one of their large tribal groups, the Brigantes, occupied the whole of the present park area. They opposed the Romans but during the second to fourth centuries AD they gradually absorbed some of the Roman culture. Their huts are sometimes grouped in small villages and their little square 'Celtic' fields are very numerous on the better drained limestone upland terraces of Craven. Three of the most impressive of their monuments are the vast area of fields and hutments at Grassington, the walled fort on the summit of Ingleborough filled with hut foundations, and the large earthwork circle, the Maiden Castle near Grinton in Swaledale.

Roman remains, roads and camps occur in the park but are not numerous. A well exca-

Pen-y-ghent (2,277ft) is actually the smallest of the Three Peaks, the other two being Ingleborough (2,373ft) and Whernside (2,419ft). They are outstanding features in the Yorkshire Dales National Park, rising spectacularly above the surrounding limestone plateau

vated, entirely accessible fort at Bainbridge, AD 80 to the beginning of the fifth century, and a temporary marching camp on Mastiles Lane, Malham Moor, reached easily on foot, are the two principal monuments within the park. Finds of coins, pottery and small articles are mainly from the Romano-British native settlements, probably got by trade or plunder. The early remains so far discussed are to be seen almost entirely on the uncultivated uplands, partly because they have escaped the destruc-tion that accompanies cultivation, and partly because the swamps and lakes and dense wood-land which filled the valley bottoms made them unusable until a more organised, numerous and experienced people colonised the valleys, in the sixth and later centuries.

A feature of the dales which is a major element among their attractions is their villages. In the larger dales these are strung out at intervals of two or three miles right along their whole length, but in the shorter dales of the west,

Dentdale and Garsdale, there is only one village centre and a regular scatter of single homesteads along the valley sides. Some villages, such as Reeth, are found clustering around a large green, while others have two rows of dwellings and farms facing one another across a long narrow street, West Witton being a good example of this. A few, but these are a minority, appear to have little formal shape, although close study will reveal some centre around which they have grown. They are all alike however, in being built on a terrace well above the river, with the flood land below being used as meadows and the old ploughed fields being situated on each side of, and immediately adjoining the village. Above them on the higher slopes the common pastures merge eventually into the moorlands. All these are variants and developments of patterns of settlement brought by the Angles and Danes, as pre-Conquest settlers.

Anglian villages have the clearest pattern and their names tend to terminate in -ley or -ton (Wensley, Middleton), while the Danish are found among them in the lower part of the dales with -by and -thorpe to distinguish them, Carperby, Thorpe and so on. The hamlets in the valley heads, in Dentdale and Garsdale and the west, are Norse, with many personal names and syllables indicating the summer settlements, and generally with a flavour entirely different from those of the eastern dales: Gunnerside (-saetr or -sett, the summer pasture), Knudmaning, Keld, Yockenthwaite. These spread over all the high valleys and ground of the west and typify the high pastures of the Norse sheep farmers of the ninth and tenth centuries.

It was the Angles and Danes who did much to create our present landscape by clearing the forest, draining the valley bottoms and breaking the waste land into cultivated fields. Much of the area around the valley heads and in the west remained as forest which the Normans kept for hunting; administered by Forest Law, there was only scattered settlement within them. These forest areas, Swaledale above Reeth, Wensleydale above Askrigg, Wharfedale above Buckden, and the great forest of Meweth, west of Ribblesdale, were not broken up and brought under cultivation until long after the Norman period.

It was the Normans and early Tudors who built the churches, and the prosperous yeomen of the seventeenth century who built stone houses to replace the earlier timber dwellings. There were not many earlier large buildings; the castles, except Bolton, and the monasteries, except Bolton Priory and the tiny fragments of Coverham, Ellerton and Marrick, are in the richer ground outside the boundaries of the park. Architecturally the park area is poor except for the interest of the vernacular building of the small domestic and farm structures. The charm of the villages lies in their great variety. No two are alike and the buildings in and around them, despite having certain common features, vary from one to another according to the ideas and taste of their owner and builder. Even the seventeenth-century farms, generally quoted as 'typical' dales buildings, have a marked individuality. The availability of stone has also added variety. In the limestone dales rubble and boulder walling, with openings and corners framed in massive cut sandstone, lintels, mullions, quoins and so on, give a character quite different from that seen in a comparable building in the northern dales where sandstone is more generally available for walling. The nature of the sandstones varies considerably and affects minor features and small ornaments.

The fields of the early settlements are sometimes marked out by ranks of lynchets or cultivation terraces, seen particularly well around Carperby and Bolton in Wensleydale, and in all upper Wharfedale and parts of Ribbles-

Sheltering behind drystone walls shepherds and sheepdog survey
their flock. Lack of government support is threatening a livelihood
which has been an integral part of the Dales scene for centuries

dale and Airedale. The medieval reversed-S-shaped rigg and furrow cultivation is equally abundant on the old common fields near most of the villages. The break up of the open fields into separate small fields by the enclosures of the late eighteenth century has spread a pattern of hedges and stone walls over all the valley landscape which we now take for granted. Except for the turnpike roads and our twentieth-century improvements there has been little change in the visual scene since ploughing ceased and the fields were turned over to pasture and dairy farming, a change which was complete by the nineteenth century.

The pattern of agriculture in the dales settled down in the eighteenth century to mixed dairy farming in the broad eastern dales with a great emphasis on cattle, and to sheep farming and hill farming in the west. Farms were small with hay meadows in the lowland, cattle grazing on the valley-side pastures and sheep on the uplands and moors. Milk, cheese, meat and wool were the staple produce while some farms specialised in breeding cattle and special strains of sheep. The changes in land usage are taking place slowly. The moors have for a few generations had multiple usage as grouse shooting and sheep grazing areas. In recent years forestry has been tried on some of the medium-high ground but without the subsidies and tax remissions from an overgenerous government, it would not be profitable and the damage it is doing would not have happened. Subsidies to the same extent could save much of the hill farming which has been such an important element in the dales scene for some centuries. The newer multiple use will be based, if we are sensible, on the great recreational potential of the park. The dales, with the beauty of their landscape and abundance of individual scenic gems, combined with an increasing awareness of their heritage of history, are attracting increasing numbers of visitors from the urban areas. Hospitality of bed-and-breakfast type as well as provision for longer holidays, particularly of family groups, could provide some supplementary incomes. There is an increasing interest in walking, and access to moorland tops is a growing demand which will have to be integrated with the interests of both farmer and sportsman. It is only such access that can allow the visitor to find the quiet and solitude which are two of the qualities that the parks were designed to preserve. This use of the moorlands can be greatly increased by making access agreements from which the owner and tenants benefit materially.

Farming has not been the only occupation in the dales. In the seventeenth to the nineteenth centuries lead and coal mining, quarrying and textiles have all for a time been important industries, and quarrying today continues on a scale vastly greater than ever before seen. The older quarries were small and numbered a few hundreds mainly for lime burning, the lime being used to improve much of the upland pasture and the limekilns in comparable numbers being an interesting component of the landscape. Other quarries became famous for stone roofing slates and a few for fine building stone. Today the giants are the limestone quarries for burned lime, for roadstone and for metallurgical flux, and some of the grits and slates for road-

stone. The area of large quarries in Wensleydale below Redmire was excluded from the park, but three areas within the park boundary have developed, and planning control is trying to confine quarrying extensions to them. Around Ingleton very old quarries in the ancient rocks beneath the limestone have been extended and modernised. In Ribblesdale there is a similar but much larger development with the addition of the largest limestone quarry only a mile or two away, while in mid-Wharfedale three limestone quarries produce up to a million tons a year and are a focus for expansion. Some of these quarries create problems of transport along what were country roads, which have been exaggerated by the closure of some railway lines and threats to others.

The lead mining industry has a history reaching back into Roman times but its period of greatest activity, when in parts of Wharfedale and Swaledale it provided the major occupation, was between the early eighteenth and the last two decades of the nineteenth centuries. On parts of the fells the remains of the lead mines are sufficiently numerous to provide abundant material and interest for any visitor with a leaning towards what is now called industrial archaeology. The housing of the miners has affected the mining villages with their high proportion of tiny cottages and with small-holding miner-farmer 'intakes' on the edge of the commons. Some of the ruined smelt mills are in very romantic and remote positions, but a few of those which are nearer the roads such as Surrender Mill and Grinton Mill have become very popular picnic places. The Surrender Mill, on Barnard Beck where the road from Low Row crosses it, is always busy with visitors enjoying the area of fine turf around the mill. Even more

---

This scene happens to be in the Yorkshire Dales – it could be in any one of the national parks. Without proper control a beauty spot can easily become an open sore

popular is the well preserved Grinton Mill, a mile out of Grinton on the Leyburn road, where the heather-clad deep valley of Cogden Beck and the mill itself lie only a hundred yards or so from the road crossing.

The people who live within the park contribute enormously through their work and life to its character. The main element is still the dalesman stock, farmers with a thousand years of tradition, and a dialect that has its roots in the speech of Norsemen, Danes and Angles. Much of its form and vocabulary is taken from the Old and Middle English which evolved from them. However, this century has slowly replaced this virile speech with something far more general and far less distinctive, a product partly of the newer schools. In the post-war decades the language has become adulterated with half-baked American slang and one can only hope that much of this will prove ephemeral and that the forthright and sterling character of a native speech and idiom will survive. The influx of older people retiring from the towns and the amazing growth in the fashion of the 'country cottage' is having its effect on the life of the dales, and the demand for the partial urbanisation of some of the villages is growing. On the farms old buildings and methods are being deserted for huge prefabricated steel-framed and asbestos-clad structures which are bringing new and alien shapes into the landscape. Farm labourers are reduced in numbers and are becoming hybrid farmer-mechanics, spending more and more time on and around tractors and machinery. Only the shepherd on the fells retains his traditional methods, and even he often has a Land Rover parked at the nearest road side.

At weekends and holidays the population within the park is many times multiplied by the visitors. Some come in by bus for walking, pot holing or for strenuous exercise on the high fells, but the removal of railways (there is no railway station within the park) and reduction of bus services is forcing the vast majority of visitors to come by car. Of these many thousands of motorists, a large proportion come out for a 'spin', to enjoy the scenery, to find a picnic spot, to spend an hour or two in a quiet lay-by before setting out on the run home. But with road improvements, and particularly with the approach of the new motorways to the verge of the park, a vast population of several millions is now within one or two hours' reach, and the implication of these motorists out on a 'spin' is frightening for those who wish to preserve something of the quiet of the countryside.

The park has an admirable network of roads which are quite adequate for the visitor but only if he is content to travel at a moderate speed and is prepared to show courteous consideration for others. The road through the length of Wensleydale is in part the old turnpike road between York by Askrigg, down Garsdale to Sedbergh and Kendal. A main way forward was by Mallerstang to Kirkby Stephen and on both the watersheds are not high, 1,100ft and 1,300ft respectively, but the fells which contain them are so high and steep that the traveller has no impression but of a deep and low level valley in the heart of high mountainous country. They are roads to be traversed slowly and enjoyed.

Wensleydale has six long tributary valleys from the south, the longest twelve and the shortest five miles long, and four of them have roads which cross passes at their head, over into Wharfedale and one into Ribblesdale, varying in height from 1,400ft to 1,900ft. Passing from Wensleydale into Swaledale the road winds carefully between the potholes of Buttertubs Pass, and there are also roads across the moors from Aysgarth and Redmire to Muker and Reeth. These roads cross a wide expanse of undulating heather moors and on fine weekends their length is dotted with happy picnic parties enjoying the sense of wide open space 'on top of the world'. In the south and west the roads are less adventurous except for the one crossing from the head of Littondale over Malham Moor into Airedale or Ribblesdale. The roads from Ingleton to Hawes and the one through Sedbergh to Kirkby Stephen are more and more used by heavy traffic, though the one through Sedbergh may get some relief as the new M6 comes into more general use.

A difficult question is that of providing for recreations which will come within the purpose of the park, to preserve and enhance the natural beauty and enable people to enjoy the countryside. Small groups are constantly advocating recreations which do not accord with this purpose. Some demand that light car, motor scooter and motorcycle trials and rallies should be allowed, since to them the quiet, twisty, hilly and narrow bylanes and green tracks appear simply as ideal trial circuits. In less extreme cases many organisations would use the park merely as a pleasant background which might attract more spectators to their games. A golf course in a lovely valley bottom would afford recreation for a very small number of privileged members, but could never be said to be helping the many thousands of visitors to enjoy the unique natural beauty. Organised sports and 'spectator events' do not come within the purpose of the designation of the park except in so far as they are a normal part of the life of the area, such as sheep sales and traditional fairs, and the village cricket or football club.

Provision for some of these organised sports in country parks outside the national parks should be sufficient to relieve some of these pressures. The line of demarcation between organised spectator sports and quiet individual sports like fishing is not always clear, but one must be drawn to safeguard the refreshing relief from the noise and bustle of urban life.

These controls are not, as is commonly believed, made simply to create a 'preserve' for a very small minority who want the park only for themselves to walk in, but are an attempt in an over-urbanised country to preserve for future generations a retreat from the stresses of industry and urban living. Such areas of quiet natural beauty have a therapeutic value for body and spirit which makes some sacrifices for their preservation a wise investment.

NATIONAL PARK

Chapter 9

NORTH YORK MOORS

Harry Mead

AREA: *553 square miles (143,221 ha)*
ALTITUDE: *0 – 1,490ft (0 – 454m)*
     Urra Moor 1,490ft (454m)
     Cringle Moor 1,427ft (433m)
     Stony Ridge 1,422ft (432m)
ADMINISTRATION: *The North York Moors National Park Committee, a separate committee of the North Yorkshire County Council, has 27 members of whom 18 are appointed by the County Council; 12 represent the North Yorkshire County Council, 2 Cleveland County Council and 1 each the District Councils of Ryedale, Scarborough, Hambleton, and Langbaurgh. 9 members are appointed by the Secretary of State for the Environment.*
POPULATION: *22,800. Thornton Dale, 1,439; Helmsley, 1,277.*
COMMUNICATIONS: *Scarborough, close to the park, is served by trains from York and Hull. The Esk Valley line serves stations within the park calling at 11 villages between Whitby and Middlesbrough, where there are connections to the main line at Darlington. At Grosmont the Esk Valley line connects with the privately operated North Yorkshire Moors Railway which runs north-south from Grosmont to Pickering.*

By road Guisborough to Castleton is 12 miles; Whitby – Grosmont 6 miles; Scarborough – Ravenscar 11 miles; Pickering – Rosedale Abbey 10 miles; Thirsk (8 miles from the A1) – Helmsley 14 miles.

Bus services are mainly on the perimeter. One frequent service from Middlesbrough reaches Whitby via the coast, and another crosses the moors from Guisborough. Whitby and Scarborough are linked by bus and receive summertime long distance services from northern towns. There is a good bus service along the southern edge of the park, between Scarborough and Thirsk, and a less frequent one through Bilsdale, between Helmsley and Stokesley.

VIEWPOINTS *with or near car parking:*
Danby Beacon (NZ 736093)
Hasty Bank (NZ 572035)
Newgate Bank (SE 563890)
Pickering Beck (SK 814908)
Robin Hood's Bay (NZ 951051)
Sutton Bank (SE 514829)

VISITOR CENTRES, MUSEUMS:
Hutton-le-Hole. Folk Museum (SE 705900)
Low Dalby. Forest Museum (SE 856874)
Midge Hall. Forest Museum (NZ 888034)
Pickering. Beck Isle Museum (SE 798842)
Whitby. Pannett Park Museum (NZ 894109)

NATIONAL PARK OFFICER, *North York Moors National Park, The Old Vicarage, Bondgate, Helmsley, Yorkshire YO6 5BP*

The North York Moors have a character magnificently their own. Sharply bounded by the sea on one side and steep escarpments on another two, here is an extensive but remarkably self-contained area of upland, broadly 40 miles by 20, threaded by some of the quietest valleys in England and with enough historic interest to last a lifetime.

In its 553 square miles are valleys as green and lovely as any in the Dales. There are villages of warm sandstone or sparkling limestone, some cradled in the valleys, others breezily sporting themselves on the moor tops. Along the coast are impressive cliffs and delightful huddled fishing villages. There are boulder-strewn becks, waterfalls, rivers rich in trout. In the Esk you can see salmon leap. If you know where to look, these 'savage' moors will even yield scenes of thatch and whitewash as snug as anything you will find in Sussex.

Around the edge is a series of the eighteenth-century market towns which are a notable feature of North Yorkshire—broad high streets, hospitable pubs, a generous air of well-being. To take one's ease in one of these market towns after a day on the hills is a highly agreeable part of the moors' experience.

The great dome of the central watershed, the Cleveland Hills, gives the region its special appeal. Few areas of England have remained so inviolate. There is a noble wildness here, capable of offering huge refreshment. If one were asked to name the chief quality of the moors perhaps this would be it: space, solitude, wildness. In North Yorkshire these combine into a landscape by which man may renew himself and begin to sense his place in the scale of things.

In late August and September the moors are ablaze with heather and ling—a purple carpet right across the forty miles from the Vale of York to the sea. Over most of the moors sheep wander at will, so that the moorland roads are edged with an emerald cushion of turf. And in Farndale each spring is greeted by daffodils arrayed a full seven miles along the River Dove.

Early man helped to shape these moors. His ever-present echoes—earthworks, burial mounds, standing circles—help to give the moors their strong spiritual appeal.

Numerous earlier civilisations now speak to us only through lonely remains like these high up in North Yorkshire. In 1937, Frank Elgee, Yorkshire's greatest archaeologist, working on Loose Howe, made a spectacular discovery—a Bronze Age burial of some importance. A body had been placed in a boat, with a second boat as cover and a third alongside. Remains of a cloak, leggings, shoes and a bronze dagger were also found. Dating from about 1600 BC these remains are in the British Museum; and a memorial to Elgee, a carved stone, can be seen by the Rosedale turning on Blakey Ridge, looking across to Loose Howe.

Human remains from other sites show exceptional development of ankle bones, probably from long periods of squatting to avoid the damp conditions. Today, scores of motorists park at Hasty Bank, near Stokesley, unaware that the site was a Bronze Age crematorium, unearthed with its blackened flue when the car park was made in 1970. It commands one of the park's best views, embracing the cone-shaped Roseberry Topping, perhaps Yorkshire's most distinctive hill, and Easby Moor, surmounted by an obelisk to Captain Cook, the explorer who was born and went to school nearby.

These discoveries, selected from many, indicate the importance of the moors as a living statement of history drawn and redrawn. Although Britain's earliest men, Paleolithic or Early Stone Age, did not penetrate to North Yorkshire, the moors have produced some of the best evidence we have of their successors—hunters of the immediate post-glacial period, about 8000 BC, who are known to have lived by a long-vanished lake near Pickering and foraged in the then thickly wooded moors. Indeed, the story of the moors is inseparable from its early people, since analysis of pollen in the peat has indicated it was they who began the clearance of the woodland, ultimately causing

Legend:

— National Park boundary

········· county boundary

- - - - road

+—+—+ railway

+—+++ railway (preservation society)

- -▲- - Rosedale railway (disused)

▲ youth hostel

★ museum/visitor centre

• town, village

········· Cleveland Way

height in metres

over 300

120 - 300

0 - 120

▲ 320 peak (height in metres)

0   kms   10

leaching of the soil, and letting in the vast stretches of heather which are so admired today.

But almost all settlement contributed to what we now enjoy. The Romans came and at Malton established the largest permanent fort in Yorkshire. From here they thrust out roads. One, known as Wade's Causeway, still strikes across the moors near Goathland, the largest stretch of preserved Roman road in Britain. Not far away, at Kirkdale, is a treasure from Saxon England—a stone sundial, on a slab 7ft long, with an inscription from which can be pieced together a good deal about Saxon settlement in the North. In 1950, the Science Museum, Kensington, took a cast of this sundial, and others exist in the Oxford Museum of History and

Science, the Manchester Museum, and in Melbourne, Australia.

After William the Conqueror's harrying of the North, monks settling in England found that the barren heaths of North Yorkshire offered both the seclusion and the large tracts of land they needed. Hence the region is especially rich in medieval monastic remains.

By the steeply wooded banks of the Rye near Helmsley stands Rievaulx Abbey, one of the most exquisite ruins in England. At nearby Old Byland fellow Cistercians founded another abbey, but because their bells were within earshot of Rievaulx, they moved a few miles to Oldstead, where another beautiful ruin still named Byland Abbey, can be seen. Over the hills is Mount Grace Priory, the finest Carthusian ruin in England: each monk lived in a separate cell, and visitors can see the elbow-shaped openings through which food could be passed without human contact. The great sheep runs established by the largest monasteries are thought to have been responsible for the final clearance of forest, leaving the moors very much as we see them today.

Medieval castles also sprang up in profusion. Three of the best are in a line across the southern edge of the park: Scarborough, Pickering and Helmsley. The shattered grey tower of Helmsley keep, overtopping the red cottage roofs, contributes greatly to the charm of one of North Yorkshire's most attractive towns.

In medieval days, before the valleys were cultivated, most routes followed the moor-tops. This has bequeathed a feature unique to Yorkshire—a legacy of old stone crosses and way-markers which match the elemental simplicity of the moors. One cross, Lille, near Fylingdales Early Warning Station, dates from before the Conquest and may be the oldest Christian monument in the North. Another cross, Young Ralph, by the roadside on Blakey Ridge, has a nick in the top from the homely custom of placing coins there for needy travellers. There is also an Old Ralph, and a white-painted Fat Betty—all much-loved occupants of the moors.

As the Middle Ages receded, the moors took part in an epic of the English countryside. With the eighteenth-century growth of London, the droving of livestock from Scotland reached its greatest height. Across the moors came huge herds. Today the western escarpment includes one of the best remaining examples of a drove road—a broad green track overlooking the Vale of York. In Thirsk a milepost shows a drover on one side, his sheep on the other, and the legend: London 220 miles.

The story of the moors is full of such inter-mingled history and beauty. While the general character is determined by the heather-clad tops, reaching 1,490ft at Urra Moor, the flanking hills and valleys are immensely varied in scenery and appeal.

To the south, the area was once covered by a sub-tropical sea. The stone bears the name Corallian Limestone. During a period of slow uplift, south-flowing rivers cut through the escarpment to carve out a long series of whale-back hills, with a steep north face and sloping tops, usually farmed, dipping to the Vale of Pickering. Known as the Tabular Hills, these form a strong east to west line and from several points can be seen like a row of lions, for ever watching the wilder moorlands to the north.

Between these guardians lie a family of sister dales, part of the wider company that gives the lie to the belief that the Moors Park is moor and nothing else. From the top of Newgate Bank, Upper Ryedale and Bilsdale can be seen laid out as from an aeroplane. The chequerwork pattern from here, with green stone-walled fields running to the brown moor, is the spirit of Yorkshire and surely the spirit of England too.

One dale, Bransdale, is so varied it carries

three names: Bransdale for the upper hill farming portion; Sleightholmedale, enfolded in woods with a little known heronry; and Kirkdale, where the Hodge Beck, in its limestone bed, sometimes disappears underground. By the church at Kirkdale roadmen in 1821 discovered a cave containing the remains of many animals, including lion, tiger, bison, elephant, hippopotamus and rhinoceros. The cave is thought to have been a hyenas' den and the remains tell an astonishing story of the animals that lived here before man, during a period in which the climate gradually changed from warm to cold before the last Ice Age.

It is around here too that Yorkshire's thatch is found, tucked away in villages like Pockley, Beadlam, and Harome. Many of the thatched houses are also of cruck construction, a timber-frame style of building that dates back to Saxon days: an example has been preserved in the Ryedale Folk Museum, Hutton-le-Hole.

Farndale, where the wild daffodils attract about 25,000 visitors every year, also shows thatch, but neighbouring Rosedale commands attention in a different way. In the nineteenth century it was the scene of a frantic ironstone boom. At the summit of Bank Top stands a row of kilns, and from here runs the bed of a remarkable railway that carried ore to blast-furnaces in County Durham.

In its eleven miles on the moors the line never once drops below 1,000ft, finally plumetting to the Tees plain by a sensational 1 in 3 decline. It was in use until 1929. In 1971 the whole of the Rosedale remains were named as one of the top ten industrial archaeological sites in the North. Swinging round the valley heads, the line is a superb walking track, with unsurpassed views down Rosedale and Farndale. It is sad to relate that a chimney associated with the mines, a famous landmark, was felled in 1972.

In its northern part this line traverses the Cleveland Hills, the backbone of the park.

There is great drama in the way the Clevelands raise themselves suddenly from the Tees plain. Four hills—Carlton Bank, Cringle Moor, Cold Moor, Hasty Bank—form a magnificent switchback ridge, complete with summit path. Britain's second official long distance walk, the Cleveland Way, 90 miles around the escarpment edges of the national park, reaches its inland climax here, and the ridge is also part of the Lyke Wake Walk, 40 miles across the roof of the moors, named after a Cleveland funeral dirge.

A key feature of the Clevelands is the Esk Valley, west of Whitby. With numerous villages—Danby, Castleton, Lealholm, Glaisdale—the valley indicates the extent to which custom and tradition survive in the moorlands of North Yorkshire. Egton Bridge has one of Yorkshire's most unusual contests, a show solely for gooseberries. It always takes place on the first Tuesday in August. Danby, like Spaunton over the moors, has a Court Leet for administering moor rights. Most of the villages support a quoits team, and on a summer's night there is no more pleasant sight, or sound, than a quoits match on the village green.

Glaciation affected this area a good deal: it is one of the classic areas in Britain for studying the subject. Three glaciers converged on North Yorkshire—from Scotland, the Lake District and Scandinavia across the North Sea. One of the wonders is Newton Dale, a miniature grand canyon between Whitby and Pickering, scoured out by water flowing from a lake locked in the Esk Valley by the coastal ice, which pushed some eight miles inland.

The North Eastern Railway ran through here. Surveyed by George Stephenson and numbering Dickens among its chroniclers, the line was closed by Beeching in 1965. Happily the North Yorkshire Moors Railway Preservation Society has restored it and regular steam and diesel services began in 1973. With over

The moors have a tamer side – cows are herded along a quiet country lane beside the ruins of the splendid Cistercian Rievaulx Abbey

7,000 members it is the largest railway preservation group in Britain—a tribute to the quality of the line. An interesting venture is the running of special geological trips with a 'resident geologist'.

Ice from the sea not only ran up the Esk. It partly overtopped the cliffs. For much of its length, the Guisborough-Whitby road marks the exact boundary: on one side cultivated land lies on boulder clay, on the other are the thin acid soils of the high moors. Underneath both lie the sandstones which are the Clevelands' characteristic material. While the southern area looks back to the time when it was a coral sea, these sandstones were laid down when a huge delta flooded the northern area; later they were uplifted to form the central plateau.

When the ice retreated, the Esk reacted vio-

lently, cutting ten gorges in a new passage to the sea. Many are followed by a train service that crosses and recrosses the river, runs through eleven villages and is undoubtedly one of the prettiest rides in the country.

In the east, the Clevelands end in the great cliffs and sandy bays which led to this portion of Yorkshire being declared a heritage coast in the Countryside Commission's 1970 report. Staithes, where some women still wear traditional fishwives' bonnets, and Robin Hood's Bay, with cliffs rich in fossils, are interesting villages, while Sandsend offers an ideal holiday beach.

In the west, around Osmotherley, the Clevelands merge with the Hambletons, in turn completing the circle with the Tabular Hills. Ice made its impact here too, creating the shy Lake

121

Gormire beneath the two huge inland cliffs of Whitestone and Roulston Scar. But where the Clevelands are challenging, the Hambletons are restful. Laurence Sterne, author of *Tristram Shandy*, lived at Coxwold in a rambling house now open to the public. Wordsworth and his sister Dorothy came over these hills and wrote in their praise. The Hambletons are also the home of a Victorian oddity—a whitewashed horse cut into the hillside above Kilburn by the local schoolmaster in 1857, now one of the symbols of Yorkshire.

All this provides abundant sources of interest. The limestone region is rich in wild flowers, one valley sheltering the May lily (*Maianthemum bifolium*), the only place in Britain where it can be considered native. Deer are spreading in North Yorkshire's forests, and in 1969 pine martens were found to be breeding in at least two places. Today parts of the moors are 'managed', mostly by controlled burning, as a reserve for grouse, and it is perhaps worth noting that an ornithologist on the Lyke Wake Walk recorded thirty-five different species of birds.

Apart from set pieces like Rievaulx Abbey, the stone and pantile village architecture is a delight and itself may hide many a masterpiece. Lastingham Church for instance has an underground crypt, among the best examples of eleventh-century architecture and perhaps part of an unfinished abbey. Pickering Church has beautifully preserved medieval wall paintings. Among the numerous vernacular curiosities one deserves to be nationally known—a refuge cut out of a huge boulder in picturesque surroundings between Littlebeck and the waterfall of Falling Foss. It has a gothic doorway, seats inside and out, and elegant lettering saying: The Hermitage, G+C 1790.

A particular pleasure are the many roads which ride the moorland ridges, with stimulat-ing views of moor and dale all around. Walking can vary from the broad solitudes of the high moors to river and woodland paths, as in Arncliffe woods, Glaisdale, or at Cropton Banks, Sinnington. Gliding has long been established at Sutton Bank and Carlton Bank, pony trekking has increased in recent years, and there are 460 official rock climbs in 18 places.

In 1971 yachting was introduced at Scaling reservoir, between Whitby and Guisborough. It is based on a £61,000 clubhouse for sailors, fishermen and birdwatchers, provided by the Tees Valley and Cleveland Water Board. Beside a main road on the edge of the moors, the site is ideal, although a similar enterprise might not be welcome in more sensitive parts of the National Park.

Since its designation in 1952, the North York Moors has not known the tourist invasion of the more popular national parks. Even today overcrowding is still largely a weekend affair, its source the conurbations of the North East, notably Teesside, and West Yorkshire. There are whole areas of the National Park, like the Siltons, a group of villages in Exmoor-like country among the Hambletons, that would scarcely recognise a tourist.

Lack of fashion through the word 'moors', plus comparative isolation from major traffic routes, has undoubtedly contributed to keeping North Yorkshire very much a Yorkshire affair. Will it always be so? The trans-Pennine motorway may be already sending more people towards the east coast, and a projected motorway linking this road with the A1 at Dishforth, a mere cockstride from the Hambletons, also has implications for the area.

As it is, North Yorkshire is finding more people beating a path to its door. Visitors to Pickering Castle rose threefold between 1968 and 1971. Founded in 1955, the Lyke Wake Walk was still little known outside its immedi-

A bridestone on the nature trail near Pickering in the North York
Moors National Park

ate district in the early 1960s. Now, over 6,000 people a year complete what is easily Britain's most popular long distance path. The Ryedale Museum attracted 2,100 visitors in 1964, 15,000 in 1968, 25,000 in 1971. The number of yachts at Whitby doubled between 1965 and 1971, and even workaday Staithes, which never saw a pleasure boat in the fifties, has had to impose a limit.

There are grounds for believing that the measures to meet the growth are not increasing as fast as the pressures. In August 1971, following a year in which the National Park Authority spent a mere £448 on camping and caravan-ning, the caravanning issue boiled over, with many caravanners near Whitby unable to find sites. Through failure to act, the authority found itself facing somewhat hysterical demands for release of sites, often with scant regard for the landscape.

The park authority has been slow, too, in developing information and interpretative services. Although there is now an information officer with go-ahead for an information centre at Sutton Bank, the authority has for too long acted as though information meant draw-ing unwelcome attention to the park. Informa-tion's role in helping people to enjoy the park

Fylingdale Moor in the North York Moors now houses the space-
age geometry of Fylingdale's Early Warning Station. It symbolises
the ever-present danger of development

purposefully, and therefore helping to reconcile the conflict between the twin aims of preservation and enjoyment, seems to have been unrecognised.

As a result tourism has developed in a lopsided way, with almost all the increase in the Helmsley-Pickering area. A great need is to make visitors aware of all the park.

A new situation was introduced in April 1974 when about 20 square miles of the park, includ-

ing Roseberry Topping, became part of Cleveland County, based on Teesside. But the whole of the park is administered by a committee of the North Yorkshire County Council, on which two Cleveland representatives sit.

In the past, the park's resources have been put to good use. Rievaulx has a long history of iron making, and a blastfurnace established there in 1577 may have been the first in the North. Levisham Moor has one of the few bloomery sites in Britain dating back to the Iron Age proper. Jet has been mined extensively, and the spoil heaps can be seen along many Cleveland valleys. Alum working even affected the shape of the headland at Sandsend Ness and the escarpment at Carlton Bank.

All this is now picturesque. But continuing exploitation is not having happy results. Until recently the park was ruthlessly sacrificed. I find it true that the Fylingdales Early Warning 'golf balls' are an eerie match for the moors—'geometry of the space age at its most alluring', as Nikolaus Pevsner says. But the rest of the paraphernalia, with radar screens and chicken-wire fences, is not. Similar vandalism was permitted by the erection of a TV mast near Whitby Abbey and another in Bilsdale.

Significantly, when the Bilsdale mast went up, the dale's vicar wrote about such artefacts 'coming to rest in the place of least resistance'. North Yorkshire has lacked friends. The threat of mineral extraction in Snowdonia provoked a national outcry. By comparison little attention was focused on the plans for three potash mines near Whitby. After government approval was given for all three, one has gone up, with dire effects on some of the highest cliff scenery in the park, at Boulby, near Staithes. One can only be thankful that development of the other two has been postponed by their promoters.

More recently, there appears to have been a change of heart at the centre. In October 1970, a company already piping natural gas to a plant at Pickering was refused permission to explore for more gas at Stoney Ridge, a very lonely part of the moors. In May 1970 a House of Commons Select Committee threw out plans for a major reservoir in Farndale. Whether this represents a genuine turning point or is an interlude before fresh assaults remains to be seen.

This much can be said: if the park has absorbed most of these intrusions, it cannot take

many more. The moors may have a highly charged atmosphere, but they are also highly susceptible. One Bilsdale TV mast, the only declaration of modern man in the high moors, may be tolerable. Two or three and the park's wilderness will be betrayed.

The park faces other threats. Of the Forestry Commission's 60,000 acres in Yorkshire, some 50,000 are in the North York Moors—about an eighth of the park's total area. Some of the Commission's recent efforts have been disappointing: it has planted conifers around a fine rim of the Clevelands above Ingleby Greenhow, a landscape that responds particularly well to the patterns of cloud and shadow that conifer forests annihilate.

One could well argue that North Yorkshire would benefit by more woodland. But despite the gains in wildlife and the provision of nature trails and forest drives, are the spreading blankets of conifers an adequate substitute for the sweep of the moors? Perhaps a greater need is for protection of the remaining hardwoods and planting of more. But although there are powers for national park authorities to own and manage woodland, and the Peak District now manages over 600 acres of small amenity woods and plants 50,000 trees a year, the North York Moors Authority spent not one penny on one tree in 1970–1.

But forestry is only part of the perplexing problem, shared by other national parks, of maintaining an upland landscape. The smallness of the farmholdings, coupled with poor soil and large areas of marginal land, are causing severe difficulties. In 1966, a study of Farndale by Leeds University concluded that it was hard to see how a decline of about half the number of men then on the land could be avoided.

It put forward an economic system based on the established pattern of livestock and root farming, that would support a two-man farm. But even this meant halving the work force and required farms of 200 acres, whereas only seven of the fifty-seven farms in Farndale exceeded even 100 acres. In Glaisdale in February 1970 only one farmer was left running sheep on the moor where there had been fifteen a few years earlier.

The role of tourism to support the upland farmer has not been fully explored. It might even be said that areas like North Yorkshire have a duty to take more visitors as part of a national strategy for relieving the more hard-pressed areas.

Certainly tourism appears to offer a brighter prospect than either decay, the advancing Tees-side commuter belt, or the second-home pheno-menon now making itself felt in Rosedale. The Farndale survey noted that, on 1966 prices of £10 per week, a guest house taking only 4 people over 12 weeks would collect £480—not much less than half the average net income. It added the interesting comment that while many farmers regarded tourism as against their voca-tion, attitudes changed as casual visitors became old friends.

Meanwhile, many farmers are fighting back by moorland reclamation. In a triangle of land between Whitby, Scarborough and Pickering, of 40,000 acres of moor that existed in 1933, 19,000 had disappeared by the early 1970s—most for forestry but increasingly for conven-tional farming. Between 1956 and 1972 one dairy farmer extended his holding from 70 acres to 1,500. Farmers can present a strong case, but if the moorland scene is held to have value, some limit will need to be set. In 1972 the park authority had to seek co-operation in stopping the plough reaching the Roman Road. In 1967 they started talking about establishing an access area to safeguard the Hole of Horcum, a natural amphitheatre near Pickering, but so far nothing has been done.

One could claim there has been too little dedication to the notion of national parks. The

North York Moors has a melancholy financial record: fourth in size, ninth in spending.

The Park Authority opposed the TV aerials and the second and third potash mines. But it was inclined to accept the Farndale reservoir as inevitable. In 1971 it rejected requests to turn the disused Whitby-Scarborough railway line into a bridleway, despite evidence inside and outside the park of wide support for the pro-posal. In 1972 it refused to find a mere £5,000 to save the Rosedale Chimney, when the Lake District Planning Board was spending £14,500 to preserve a mill in Eskdale. Today the Rose-dale kilns are decaying, although the interest in them emphasises that they call for preservation as much as a medieval abbey.

These failures are crucial, for they are failures to extend the area's recreational interest and opportunities, in the spirit of the national parks. An urgent need now is to waymark the best of the network of paths—one of the main ways in which visitors can be encouraged to make fuller use of the park.

Perhaps a change could be detected in 1972–3 when the county council put up £57,250 for the now restored North Yorkshire Moors Rail-way and expressed an interest in creating a day-visitor centre, costing £105,000, in Eskdale. The money for the railway, enabling trains to run eighteen miles instead of six and reach the market town of Pickering, is to be repaid by the Preservation Society.

The visitor may be regarded as part of a hostile horde or as a person entitled to the pleasure and enrichment which the national parks can give. After more than twenty years the North York Moors National Park, despite its problems and its losses to industry, remains impressively intact over the greater part of its area. The long freedom from the car means there is still time to apply the high standard of care by which its qualities can be enjoyed, harmlessly, by those who come.

Chapter 10

NORTHUMBERLAND

J. S. Allen

AREA: *398 square miles (103,079ha)*

ALTITUDE: *184–2,674ft (56–815m)*

The Cheviot 2,674ft (815m)

Hedgehope Hill 2,343ft (714m)

Windy Gyle 2,032ft (616m)

ADMINISTRATION: *The Northumberland National Park and Countryside Committee, a separate committee of the Northumberland County Council, has 27 members of whom 18 are appointed by the County Council; 15 represent the County Council and 1 each the District Councils of Alnwick, Berwick upon Tweed, and Tynedale. 9 members are appointed by the Secretary of State for the Environment.*

POPULATION: *2,400. Elsdon, 198; Stonehaugh, 184.*

COMMUNICATIONS: *Newcastle upon Tyne is on the main line from London to Edinburgh and has excellent links with other large cities. Pay trains operate along the Tyne Valley south of the park on the line from Newcastle to Carlisle, serving Hexham and Haltwhistle, and less frequently Haydon Bridge and Bardon Mill.*

Newcastle (NE Airport) is less than one hour's flying time from London, and services to and from the Continent are increasing.

By road Newcastle (which is on the A1) to Elsdon is 33 miles, to Byrness 42 miles; Hexham – Housesteads 12 miles; Jedburgh – Carter Bar 11 miles; Wooler – Kirknewton 6 miles.

An experimental 22 seater midibus service was introduced in 1974 to link the main Roman sites on Hadrian's Wall during the summer holidays. It connects with trains on the Newcastle to Carlisle line and bus services from Hexham to Haltwhistle.

VIEWPOINTS *with or near car parking:*

Garleigh Moor, Simonside Hills (NZ 038997)

Steel Rigg, Roman Wall (NY 751676)

Winters Gibbet and road to Elsdon (NY 963908)

NATIONAL PARK INFORMATION CENTRES:

Byrness. 9 Otterburn Green; tel Otterburn 622 (NT 764026)

Ingram. The Old School House; tel Powburn 248 (NU 020163)

Once Brewed. Military Road, Bardon Mill; tel Bardon Mill 396 (NY 752669)

Mobile.

OTHER VISITOR CENTRES, MUSEUMS:

Natural History:

Kielder. Border Park Museum (NY 633934)

Lewisburn. Field Museum (NY 651904)

Roman Antiquities:

Chesterholm. Vindolanda (NY 770664)

Chollerford (near). Chesters Museum (NY 908704)

Corbridge. Corstopitum (NY 984648)

Housesteads. Vercovicium (NY 790688)

NATIONAL PARK OFFICER, *Bede House, All Saints Office Centre, Newcastle upon Tyne NE1 2DH*

Northumberland National Park is the most northerly in Britain, and like the adjoining Border Forest Park, could well have extended into Scotland if the 1949 Act had embraced that country. Indeed, it lies between two historic boundaries—the Scottish Border and Hadrian's Wall.

Its varied scenery is of rare quality, not easy to define. The park has few popular picture card 'beauty spots', no mountains comparable in height or extent with those of Snowdon or the Cairngorms, no lakes comparable in size or range of scenery with those of the Lake District, nor cliffs and coves in dramatic conjunction with sea and sky like those of Cornwall and Gower.

Its claims lie elsewhere: in the variety of form and colour of its hills and valleys, the wide horizons, a partnership between broad valleys and vast skyscape, and in its rich flora and fauna. Add to this a sense of remoteness, a romantic history, and something of the park's enthralling qualities will be apparent as they were to, among others, Walter Scott, the Northumberland Trevelyans and John Dower.

The park's long and irregular boundary was designated in 1956, after much careful thought, and after omitting *a* the unsurpassed coast (later designated an area of outstanding natural beauty) as this would have entailed including a considerable area of flat farmland, and the A1 trunk road, *b* most of the Roman Wall, as this would have involved Cumberland on the west, already a major partner in the Lake District National Park and, on the east industrial Tyneside, and *c* Kielder Forest already owned and administered by the Forestry Commission. The park covers 398 square miles and is some 40 miles long from north to south and averages 10 miles across; for convenience of description it may be divided into five sections, namely the Cheviots, the Simonside Hills, the North Tyne Valley, Redesdale, and the Roman Wall.

The Cheviot Hills, whose green slopes occupy the highest and most northerly part of the park, include the central dome of the Cheviot (2,674ft), and the valleys of rivers which rise on its slopes. The College and Harthope Burns

and the Breamish find their way to the sea via the Till, and the Coquet runs between the Cheviots and the Simonside Hills to the east coast.

South of the Cheviot, the Coquet and the Simonside Hills form a quite different landscape. The peaceful valley of the Coquet lies near Rothbury and above it are the Fell Sandstone ridges of Simonside and Harbottle Hills. Here the heather and bracken slopes are in sharp contrast to the grass of the Cheviots. Here too is the valley of the Grasslees burn, well wooded in contrast to the sandstone crags.

To the south-west of Coquetdale lies the upland valley of the River Rede, the scene of many Border skirmishes, since it provided the traditional hill route to and from Scotland. The centre of the Rede Valley is Otterburn, the scene of a famous battle bearing its name, and the inspiration for the ballad of Chevy Chase. In the upper part of Redesdale are large Forestry Commission plantations and the forest village of Byrness. Elsdon, lying between Coquetdale and Redesdale, perhaps the most interesting village in the park, is one of the few green villages in the area.

The North Tyne Valley, more sheltered than Redesdale, is a well populated sector of the park centred about Bellingham and has well cultivated farmlands.

The fifteen-mile-long section of the Roman Wall which dominates the southern area of the park, includes some of the best preserved and most spectacular portions of the Wall. Much of it crosses the Whin Sill, a basalt extrusion.

These areas, differing in their landscape, have a human history stretching from man's early occupation of Britain to the conclusion of the Border raids and Jacobite risings. The area played a vital part in the long period of Roman occupation and the entry of Christianity to Britain, and yet remained sparsely populated and restless long after most of Britain had developed

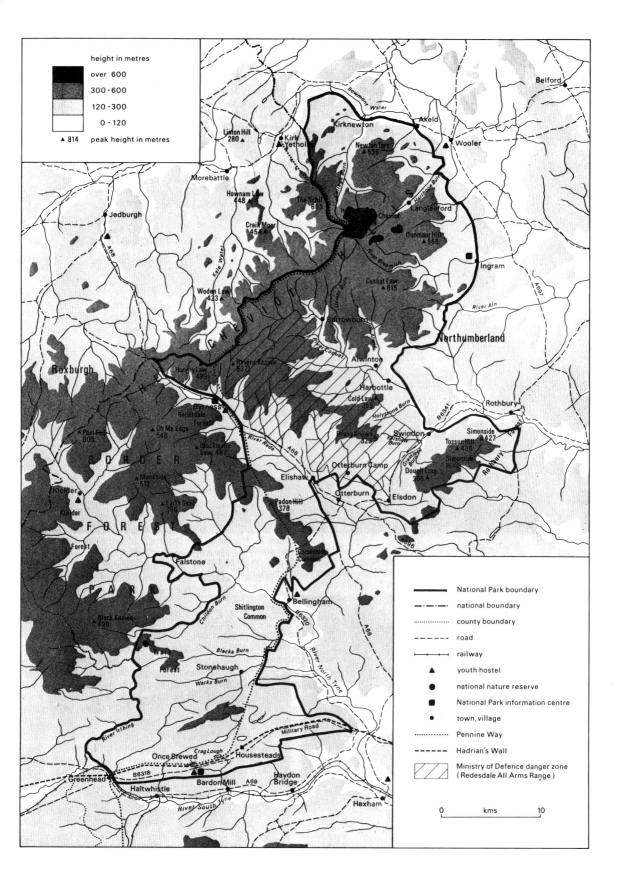

height in metres

over 600

300 - 600

120 - 300

0 - 120

▲ 814   peak height in metres

Belford

Bowmont Water

Kirknewton

Akeld

Linton Hill 280 ▲

Kirk Yetholm

Newton Tors 536 ▲

Wooler

Morebattle

Hownam Law 448 ▲

The Schil 603 ▲

Cheviot

Harthope Burn

Langleeford

Jedburgh

Craik Moor 454 ▲

Cheviot

Dunmoor Hill 586 ▲

Ingram

River Breamish

Kale Water

Woden Law 423 ▲

Cushat Law 615 ▲

River Aln

River Coquet

C H E V I O T

Barrowburn

Usway Burn

Alwinton

Northumberland

Roxburgh

Hungry Law 499 ▲

Ravens Knowe 527 ▲

Harbottle

Cold Law

Holystone Burn

Rothbury

Byrness

Redesdale Forest

Oh Me Edge 548 ▲

Rosly Knowe 326 ▲

Swindon

Kershope Burn

Simonside 427 ▲

B6341

Peel Fell 600 ▲

Blackman's Law 457 ▲

River Rede

A68

Tosson Hill 436 ▲

Simonside Hills

Rothbury Forest

B O R D E R

Monkside 512 ▲

Elishaw

Otterburn Camp

Grasslees Burn

Dough Crag 386 ▲

Kielder

Kielder

Earl's Seat 396 ▲

Otterburn

Elsdon

F O R E S T

Padon Hill 378 ▲

Forest

Falstone

A696

P A R K

Corsenside Common

Black Knowe 490 ▲

Wark Forest

Childon Burn

Shitlington Common

Bellingham

B6320

River North Tyne

A68

Blacka Burn

Stonehaugh

Warks Burn

River Irthing

Military Road

Crag Lough

Once Brewed

Housesteads

Greenhead

B6318

Bardon Mill

A69

Haydon Bridge

Haltwhistle

River South Tyne

Hexham

National Park boundary

national boundary

county boundary

road

railway

▲ youth hostel

● national nature reserve

■ National Park information centre

• town, village

Pennine Way

Hadrian's Wall

Ministry of Defence danger zone (Redesdale All Arms Range)

0   kms   10

a settled urban and rural society.

Northumberland National Park is still sparsely populated, and its small villages and scattered hamlets present problems of education and rural employment; many farms are so isolated that the ordnance maps indicate the name of a single farmstead, where in other counties considerable villages would appear. Its resident population is some 2,400.

Nevertheless, the park is easily approached by rail and road and by air. Unlike some other areas of natural beauty, no major industrial route passes through the park. It may be reached by road from north or south via the A1, the main link between London and Edinburgh, or the A68, part of which passes through the park, or from east or west by the B6318, called the Military Road, constructed or at least conceived by General Wade in the eighteenth century, and which incidentally is an excellent way to visit the Roman Wall, the North Tyne and Redesdale Valleys. Entry to the park can be made through small market towns such as Wooler, Rothbury, or Bellingham, but much of the park especially in the north is crossed only by forest roads or rough tracks.

In the following pages the impact of nature and man upon the park, the present-day life of its people, and opportunities for enjoyment in the park, are further, but all too briefly, examined.

The park and its landscape today are the result of formative influences going back at least some 300 million years; but in more recent times, man's impact has been increasingly intrusive. These influences may be traced first through its geology and climate, and later by man's occupation.

The rock foundation is, of course, the basic influence on the scenery, the most ancient rocks being older than those of Europe, but younger than the oldest in Britain, which are to be found in the West. The Cheviot stems from the Old Red Sandstone lava, through which a great granite intrusion took place, to form the top of the Cheviot of today.

The central portion of the park is dominated by the Simonside-Tosson range. Here are the Fell Sandstones whose characteristic features are seen where the crags face the Cheviot, with more gently falling ground on the other side of the hills. Tosson reaches 1,447ft, Simonside 1,409ft, and Harbottle 900ft at Cold Law.

The scenery changes again when it reaches the Rede and North Tyne Valleys, where fine moorland, cut into by the two valleys, is found. The moorland reaches heights of around 1,000ft at Otterburn, the Wannies, Corsenside Common and Shitlington Common. The area is composed of a succession of sandstones of the Lower Limestone Group, which includes the famous Blaxter Quarry, but the valleys have cut down into the more fertile shaly Scremerston Coal Group.

An intrusive quartz dolerite, known as the Whin Sill, crosses the county from west of Hexham through the National Park, including some of the finest sections of the Roman Wall, and appears at Bamburgh and the Farne Islands. In this southern section of the park, ridges of sandstone with lesser ridges of limestone developed within the Middle Limestone Group.

The drainage system is determined by the geology described above, conspicuously so in the Cheviot, from which the tributaries of the Kale and the Bowmont, in Scotland, drain westwards, the College Burn northwards, the Harthope Burn north-east, and the Breamish eastwards.

The county does not share with its western neighbour Cumbria, nor the west of Scotland, the full advantage of the benign influence of the Gulf Stream. Nevertheless, it does enjoy a south-west prevailing wind, and shares with London a rainfall well below that of its western

The Northumberland National Park has yet to experience the large-scale invasion of visitors so common further south but solitude has its repercussions for farmers

national park neighbours. Moreover, when the east wind blows over the county, it has arrived via the sea, and not directly from the Continent, as is the case in Kent or Essex. Thus, although temperatures are never exhaustingly high in the National Park, there is a very considerable amount of unclouded and sunny weather to be enjoyed in both summer and winter.

The activities of local groups of enthusiasts such as the Northumberland Wildlife Trust, as well as national societies, help to encourage an appreciation of the significance of wildlife in our materialistic and over-urbanised society. The National Park offers large areas in which nature may be studied and where the habitats of both flora and fauna have undergone changes from time to time. The increasing rate of change creates increasingly difficult problems of conservation.

Change, however, is not a newcomer, for in earlier periods much of the now bare hillsides or heather-clad moors was prehistoric forest, with Scots Pine, birch, hazel, alder, oak, elm, rowan, or ash, only sparse remnants of which survive to this day. Without doubt the change was brought about by the spread of peat in the wetter and warmer periods of pre-history. Wildlife also has undergone changes, following natural changes of vegetation and of climate. The bear, the wolf, and the wild-cat have disappeared, and various species of birds have been threatened with extinction.

Two less natural, but nevertheless inevitable reasons for the loss of natural forest followed the Anglo-Saxon invasions, when felled forest provided the major building material and when grazing prevented the natural regeneration of woodland, whilst favouring the growth of grass or heather. This latter activity further accelerated when, following the more settled times resulting from the Union of England and Scotland in 1603, open-range grazing of sheep developed.

Much of the Cheviot is grass covered with peat vegetation crowning the high hills. In the wet rocks, such as at Henhole, one finds alpine scurvy-grass, in the drier peat of blanket bog heather predominates, while in the wetter peat cotton sedges are found.

On outcrops of andesite, a rich brown earth with high organic content, a wide range of the tall herbs flourish. The best examples of relict woodland occur in Coquetdale, standards of upland oak and junipers at Holystone Burn, ash with hazel at Alwinton, and the now rare alder in Grasslees Burn. The hay meadows of the North Tyne are botanically interesting because the abundance of plants indicates a woodland origin of the 'haughs'. On spate-scoured river gravels on the Rede and North Tyne are four localities for *Eleocharis austriacca* newly added to British flora.

The Border Mires sites, selected by the Nature Conservancy, and watched over by the Northumberland Wildlife Trust, support characteristic sphagnum bog vegetation. The Whinstone escarpment, at the Roman Wall section of the park, may be described as the counterpart of the Border Mires flora; here rosebay willowherb is common and in places where limestone is exposed below the whinstone, the rock rose appears. The lakes in the hollows below the escarpment represent a further facet of the botany, resplendent with water plants of many kinds.

Three large mammals are found in the park. The fox and badger, so different in their personal habits, are found everywhere. But the roe deer find the new conifer woodlands attractive, and are humanely culled at intervals by the Forestry Commission's selected marksmen. The shy red squirrel may be seen in suitably mature woodland. Reptiles such as the viper, common lizard, and slow worm, are to be found in heath cover, but never in abundance.

Birds are limited to special habitats. The dipper, goosander, ring ouzel and grey wagtail are to be seen on mountain streams, whereas the open moorland supports the curlew (the park's elegant emblem), short-eared owl and the red grouse, and on the tops the golden plover nests. Black game will be found in young conifer woodland, as will redstarts in company with several different kinds of titmouse. But birdlife abounds especially in valley bottoms where arable farming is possible. Here, where the rivers are slower, heron are not infrequent today, and the kingfisher has made a dramatic comeback following the devastating winter of 1963.

Man's arrival in the area of Northumberland National Park was later than elsewhere in England. A small group of Middle Stone Age men may have arrived in the fifth millennium. Neolithic man, about 4000 BC, left evidence of his occupation in the form of polished stone implements around Coquetdale and Redesdale. At the end of the Neolithic Age and the beginning of the Bronze Age, about 1800 BC, invasion of the Tyne by the so-called Beaker folk resulted in settlements in central Coquetdale, and especially Rothbury, where their characteristic ceramics were found. They also served to open up trade for the tradesmen of the early Bronze Age.

During the Bronze Age, the local population grew steadily, and it would appear that the Beaker folk were absorbed by the indigenous native stock. Bronze Age people settled in Coquetdale and on the left bank of the Tyne, and their barrows are associated not only with menhirs and groups of standing stones, but also with quantities of 'cup and ring' motifs on rocks and boulders, especially a fine series near Lordenshaw among the Fell Sandstones. The precise dating of standing stones is difficult to establish, but remains of two of large diameter may be seen at Threestone Burn east of Hedgehope on the Cheviot, and near Hethpool in the College Valley.

The Bronze Age persisted long in the county, and there is still conjecture regarding the origin of the large groups of timber-built settlements and fortified sites which preceded Roman occupation; Yeavering Bell is the largest known site, covering some thirteen acres. Little, too, is known of the pattern of agriculture of these pre-Roman centuries, nor the effects of the fluctuating fortunes of the imperial frontier.

The final quarter of the first century BC witnessed the Roman occupation of the north of Britain. Communications extending northwards from Chester and from York were linked by east-west routes, the easiest being through the Tyne Gap. The Stanegate, the east-west route from Corbridge (and perhaps from South Shields) to Carlisle, is older than the Wall and lies within the park. It had forts at Corbridge, Chesterholm (its British name, Vindolanda, was used by the Romans), Nether Denton, and Carlisle.

The Wall itself, planned under Hadrian in AD 122, extended from Wallsend on the Tyne to Bowness on the Solway, in Cumbria, and some fifteen miles of the finest remains of its $72\frac{1}{2}$ (80 Roman) miles lie within the park.

Hadrian's Wall, providing good communications between east and west, enabled a comparatively small garrison to control the frontier defences by signaller-soldier observation. The Wall consisted of seventeen forts of which Housesteads is perhaps the best preserved, each with a north and south gate, and further reinforced with milecastles set 1,620yd (one Roman mile) apart, linked by wall composed of rubble faced with coursed sandstone, 10ft thick and 15ft high. A signallers' turret spanned the north gate of each milecastle, and between every two milecastles were two equally spaced signal towers. This continuous line of defence was strengthened on its north side by a V-shaped ditch, 12ft deep and 27ft wide. On the south, wherever possible, a wide, flat-bottomed ditch, called by antiquarians the Vallum, was dug out of the earth and occupied the middle of a 100ft-wide cleared strip of ground.

North of the Wall are three outposts of interest, one at Risingham (on West Woodburn), one at Elishaw near the northern crossing of the Rede by Dere Street, and one at High Rochester.

The Wall, served by supply depots, with the forts, each a small town, formed a frontier society complete with dwellings, shops, temples, granaries, and public buildings. It has a history too long to recount here, but it served its purpose almost continuously until the final withdrawal of the legions in the fifth century AD. In spite of destruction and neglect, it remains a unique monument.

Indeed, the visitor cannot but be conscious of the power which this survival from a great empire can still exercise over the imagination, although few would today go so far as Pro-

Abandoned during the final withdrawal of the legions in the fifth
century AD, Hadrian's Wall, here snaking across Hotbank Crags,
remains a unique monument to a dead civilisation

copius, the sixth-century historian, who saw the
Wall 'dividing a garden to the south from death
to the north'.

The years from the early fifth century, when
the Romans finally left Britain, to the eleventh
century, were full of incident and strife, but left
little visual evidence within the park. One
reason for this is that the upland areas did not
appeal to the raiders who, when they did settle,
appeared to prefer river valley sites such as the
Coquet and Glen, and later the Tyne Gap,
rather than the uplands, or else settlements along

the established Roman roads. Another reason is
that during this period timber was the dominant
building material, as indicated in the palace of
Yeavering (possibly begun in the reign of
Aeoelfrith at the beginning of the sixth century).
On the other hand, since sites are difficult to
locate, it is possible that settlement was greater
than is known.

The earldom of Northumbria was the suc-
cessor to the earlier kingdom of Northumbria,
and its status had a profound influence on the
government of the area after the Norman Con-

quest, for most of the area consisted of 'liberties' or 'franchises', each enjoying considerable independence. During medieval times, most of the present national park area lay either in the Liberty of Redesdale or in the Liberty of Tynedale. The headquarters of the former were first the great castle at Elsdon and later the castle of Harbottle, which guarded the route into Scotland. There is no evidence to indicate that either Redesdale or Tynedale was exceptionally lawless before the end of the thirteenth century. But during the fourteenth, fifteenth and sixteenth centuries, when there was long strife between England and Scotland, 'ritstall' (Redesdale) became the word for wildness and thieving. This was the turbulent era with which the famous Border ballads were concerned. These were long transmitted simply by word of mouth, but later they started to appear as broadsheets, and ultimately came out in full published form in the eighteenth century. The ballads are the means by which these restless years can best be appreciated.

The inquiring visitor doubtless will be intrigued by place-names, whether they describe a homestead, river, valley, hill-top, or record a Border battle. A name may be Celtic, Roman, Anglo-Saxon, Norman, or medieval in origin. If he is not already versed in place-names, he will learn that 'laws' is a mountain or hill or just a mound, that 'Byrness' was a barrow on a ness or headland, that a 'hope' is a small, enclosed, or 'blind' valley, a little narrower than a 'dene', less precipitous than a 'cleugh' (or ravine), and less liable to flooding than a 'haugh'. (The latter means the flat land by a stream.) He will also discover that Rothbury is the modern name for Hrotha's stronghold—a Scandinavian settlement—and that many a farmstead still carries the name, in one form or another, of its first occupant.

The unsettled conditions under which the Border long existed following the departure of the Roman legions were not conducive to development of a progressive architecture. Indeed, for many centuries building, whether domestic or ecclesiastical, was dominated by the need for defence against fellow men or the weather. The visitor will therefore look in vain for the rich craftsmanship and materials which reflect the wealth and social stability of the Cotswolds, or other comparatively fortunate counties in the South. But he will find a skilfully arranged array of fortified buildings, some of which changed as security improved. Of the many castles which were built in Northumberland, only two were in the park—at Elsdon and Harbottle. For the greater castles, one must visit Bamburgh or Alnwick. But many towers, such as at Dally, Tarset, and Thirlwell, were given the courtesy title of castle. Of the smaller towers, remains may be seen at Biddlestone, Great Tosson, and the one-time rectory at Elsdon.

The defensive pele houses or pele towers have survived more or less as dwellings, as at High Rochester and Ridge End, or as byres or barns, as at Whitlees and Gatehouse. The most interesting, however, largely because they have escaped more recent restoration and the early farmhouse site has not been disturbed, may be seen at Highshaw Iron House and Low Cleughs.

The more settled times following the Union with Scotland witnessed the adaptation of fortified houses, such as Clennell near Alwinton, and Hesleyside near Bellingham.

There are comparatively few churches in the area of the National Park; the great church-building era ended in the thirteenth century in Northumberland. Attempts to redress this took place in the nineteenth century, but not always with success. The churches in the Cheviots area often have an open bell turret on the west gable, as at Elsdon, Alwinton, Alnham, and Holystone.

Sandstone was used for building throughout the county until recent times, including the earliest building by the Romans, who used sandstone even where the great Wall crossed the Whin Sill. The simplest farmhouse, often single-storied, with byre adjoining, was of sandstone, with laminated stone roofing.

Northumberland National Park has for centuries been dominated by agriculture. Much of the farming is above 1,000ft where 2,000 acres is an economic unit for sheep. Four-fifths of the farms are more than 300 acres in extent, usually consisting of 'outbye' upland for extensive sheep grazing, and 'inbye' land around the farmstead. Apart from the effect of large scale afforestation, the wholesale decline of farms with untenanted farmhouses, which occurred elsewhere, has not yet taken place within the park.

The differing nature of upland grazing has encouraged the development of various breeds of sheep. To the north of the park will be found the White-Faced Border or South Country Cheviot ewe, bred here and grazing on the 'white' land, that is where grass covers the land. On poorer grassland, or where heather dominates—'black' land—the horned Scotch Black-Faced ewe will be found, whereas just south of the Roman Wall country, the popular Border Leicester or Blue-Faced Leicester is used for crossing with Cheviot. But whatever breed of sheep one sees it will always be tended by the Northumberland farmer and his shepherd, whose pure and musical dialect speech welcomes the appreciative visitor. In spite of changing conditions, the shepherd and his indispensable dog (usually a black and white Border Collie) still form part of the scenery, and it is not surprising to find sheepdog trials a feature of the sporting calendar, or that the first sheepdog trials in Britain took place at Byrness in Redesdale in 1879.

But hill farming has undergone many changes, especially as a result of the Hill Farming Act of 1946, a significant year in the history of human and animal population distribution, for the New Towns Act also was passed in the same year. The effect of the Hill Farming Act was to increase the number and kinds of cattle on Britain's uplands. Today, the traditional beef breeds and crosses—the Herefords, Angus, and Galloways—are varied by the introduction of the Friesian, the Charollais, and soon, no doubt, the Limousin and other foreign breeds. Since hill land in Northumberland has a pH of about 4, which is highly acidic, the choice for the future lies between improving the land by drainage and other means, or risk an increasing wilderness.

To this isolated rural society two new kinds of resident-cum-visitor have been added. First the armed forces occupy a considerable area of the National Park, the Redesdale All Arms Range which lies between Redesdale and Coquetdale. The other newcomer is also a phenomenon of this century. Whereas the railway, largely resulting from inventions in the county, brought prosperity to Britain, it did not bring to the park the expected degree of affluence (although Hexham, Wooler and Rothbury expanded). Northumberland had to await the advent of the motorcar to make the park readily accessible to visitors of all ages, and has consequently begun to face the demand for a 'second home'. Nevertheless, demand has by no means yet reached the embarrassing proportions of many other areas, whether seaside or inland. But the growing popularity of the country cottage, or the less traditional chalet or stationary 'caravan' on a permanent site, will certainly create pressures here, although it is to be hoped with less intensity than elsewhere. In the meantime, the Forestry Commission—a 'dual purpose' Commission indeed—has provided a limited site for chalets adjoining its forest village at Stonehaugh in the Wark Forest.

The peaty brown waters of the River Rede rush across stones and boulders near Otterburn. The Northumberland Border country is the setting of many notable ballads.

The impact of change on the park has been relatively small. The largest single area of the county already affected by afforestation, at Kielder, was excluded from the designated park, but afforestation nevertheless offers the greatest foreseeable opportunity (or threat—according to one's point of view) of change. The county council is of the opinion that afforestation should in future be considered as 'development' and so subject to control like building, but would accept as 'permitted development' fairly generous planting of shelter belts. Should economic policy be in favour of maximum agricultural production revolutionary improvement of hill land could follow, and indeed is foreshadowed in the fencing of upland farms in south-west England.

Apart from defence and afforestation activities, the park has been fortunate. No major claims in the form of defence warning systems, no nuclear power stations nor pumped storage schemes for electricity generation, no devastatingly large quarries, nor, until recently, any vast reservoirs appeared on the programme of technological progress. Nevertheless, the park is threatened by depopulation, for modern farming here, as elsewhere, rarely offers adequate opportunities for the younger generation whose education is primarily directed towards urban tastes and skills.

Undoubtedly the best way to explore upland country is on foot, and this is especially true of Northumberland. The character of its landscape ensures that walking along ridge routes such as the central sector of the Roman Wall, or Clennell Street from Yetholm to Alwinton, one can enjoy extensive views, and often the firmest ground; one should also follow the burnsides and rivers in the same way, to get most satisfaction out of the experience.

The Cheviots provide beautiful scenery and interesting ancient camp sites, while walking

through Redesdale and Coquetdale means a journey full of changing views and colours. Upper Redesdale is, however, under Forestry Commission planting, and although the Commission most commendably sets out to make the forest interesting and enjoyable, planting limits access and views.

The more sheltered valley of the North Tyne is likewise delightful walking country; here will be found attractive farmhouses and well farmed valley bottoms, above which rough grassland and heather moor may be explored.

Without a doubt, the Roman Wall country is more universally known and attracts more visitors than other parts. Not only the Wall itself but the rolling countryside and the small Northumbrian lakes which lie below may be reached on foot, and many fine views obtained even by simply following the road, from Housesteads camp to Crag Lough. It is also worth remembering that almost a quarter of the 250 miles of the Pennine Way is in Northumberland, and in much of the country that it traverses there are magnificent views.

But not everyone can undertake walking adventures of this magnitude and many must depend on other forms of transport. Alas! exploration of the park by public transport is limited since the closure of the scenic North Tyne railway and reduction of rural bus services.

For the motorist, however, there are excellent roads. First there is the A68 which links the Roman Wall to Carter Bar on the Scottish Border; secondly, running parallel with the River North Tyne is the road from Bellingham to Falstone, and thirdly, there is the 'Military Road', the B6318, which runs from Chollerford to the Cumbria border. The Cheviot, however, is different. For parts of the College valley a permit is required as sections of the road are private, and, of course, further restrictions are imposed within the Redesdale All Arms Range.

Most traditional field sports are available for those who can enjoy them. Nine registered packs of foxhounds in the county hunt in the National Park, the College Valley claiming to dispatch 100 foxes in a season. In addition, the hare is hunted by beaglepacks. The park also offers attractive pony trekking country and there are four centres available.

Fishing is generally private, but some local hotels and angling clubs offer facilities to visitors. In the Coquet some of the cheapest salmon fishing in the country may be obtained, and pike are found in a number of lakes. Sailing, permitted on Greenlee lough, is limited to members of a sailing club.

Rock climbing is not on the scale of the more famous British centres but can be enjoyed in various parts of the park: on the basalt Whin Sill near the Roman Wall, on the sandstone outcrops of Simonside, and on the Cheviot granite. Perhaps the best and most extensive is to be found at Crag Lough, and High Sheils Crag has much more than local fame.

To assist the visitor a warden system and an information service have been established. Three information centres have been provided at Ingram, Byrness and Once Brewed serving respectively, the Cheviot, Redesdale and the Roman Wall areas.

This then, is the most northerly national park. An extensive area of remote hills and wide valleys, home of Border country legends and former outpost of a great empire, it is a connoisseur's country and, as yet, still 'far from the madding crowd'.

Chapter 11

SCOTLAND

John Foster

Many people ask why there are no national parks in Scotland. It is a fair question, in a country which possesses such a great diversity of scenery in the 30,000 square miles of its mainland and islands. It seems even more extraordinary when one considers that it attracted 7 million visitors from beyond its borders in 1972, and tourism brought £215 million into its economy.

To understand why, one needs to dig back into history and, in doing so, to remember that the pressures on the Scottish countryside over the years have never been as great as in England. Nominally, the 5 million or so resident Scots today could claim 3·6 acres apiece if Scotland were parcelled out in individual plots; the comparable figure for England is less than 0·7 acres. Scotland still has space—a commodity becoming increasingly precious in many parts of Western Europe.

The span of history which provides a background to understanding the situation today begins with the Access to Mountains (Scotland) Bill 1884—a mere 90 years ago in time, but a world away in every other respect. That Bill was promoted by James Bryce, later to become British Ambassador in Washington where he took a great interest in American national parks. Bryce failed to obtain for the public right of access to the mountain land of Scotland, despite his canny poaching safeguard that access should only be during the hours of daylight! However, his effort marked a quickening of public interest in outdoor recreation, soon to become closely linked with a parallel interest in conservation, which together were to produce a spate of voluntary bodies with a lively concern for the environment.

Although interest in recreation developed steadily in Scotland, it did so at a slower rate than in England. For one thing, people on foot have traditionally had a relative freedom of movement on the Scottish hills and over the years those who found their way out of the crowded towns of the central belt into the Arrochar Highlands and the Trossachs to the Grampians and beyond, were able to move about with little hindrance, provided they behaved responsibly and recognised the sensitivities of sporting interests, particularly during the deer-stalking season. The motorcar did not penetrate far into this countryside in any numbers until the 1920s; hills like the Rest and Be Thankful, and the Devil's Elbow were not so named without good reason!

A few areas of Scotland appeared on the Great Britain map of suggested national parks which accompanied a Government report on the subject in 1932, but it was not until 1945, in the flood of post-war reconstruction, that anything really significant occurred. A Scottish report on national parks (the Ramsay Report) recommended five areas as suitable for national parks, all of them located in the central and north-west Highlands, with a further three areas to be reserved for later consideration. The eight areas took in 2,630 square miles of high quality landscape; almost 9 per cent of Scotland.

These first selections were confirmed two years later and in 1949 a joint report of two Government committees incorporated proposals for nature reserves as well.

While England and Wales in the early post-war years moved towards national parks legislation, there was little parallel activity in Scotland. Since access to the countryside was still easy and relatively free, there was no significant call from landowners to control it nor from recreational interests to exploit it. Development pressures outside the central belt were still only slight and threats to the traditional landscape character of the Highlands and the Southern Uplands were not evident. Furthermore, the idea of public ownership of land in national parks ('... to be owned or controlled by the Nation ...' as the Ramsay Report put it) did not appeal in some quarters and, it was well known at the time, would have been strongly resisted. In the event, it was not seen as necessary in 1949 to apply to Scotland the powers of the National Parks and Access to the Countryside Act, apart from those sections dealing with nature conservation, under which subsequently some 41 national nature reserves have been established and are today under the care of the Nature Conservancy Council.

Strictly there is not really a great deal more to the national park story in Scotland, but of activities concerned with cherished land, and provision for informal recreation in the countryside, there is much more to be said. It was a fortunate circumstance in 1948 which decided the Secretary of State to identify the five main areas of the Ramsay Report in a National Park Direction Area Order, thereby enabling him subsequently to influence the scale and nature of new development and changes in the use of land permitted in them. Under the Countryside (Scotland) Act, 1967, the Secretary of State now has power to designate, for similar purposes, further areas of particular beauty as areas of special planning control; this he does with advice from the Countryside Commission for Scotland.

During the 1960s in Scotland, no less than elsewhere in Britain, 'The Countryside in 1970' movement stimulated constructive thought about the future. A study group on Countryside Planning and Development in Scotland reported to the second Countryside in 1970 conference in 1965 and argued the case for setting up a countryside commission for Scotland, suggesting a range of powers and duties which subsequently greatly influenced the shape of the Countryside (Scotland) Act two years later. During the same period a group of technical experts studied the Cairngorm area and produced a widely acclaimed report for the '... development of (its) tourist potential and the safeguarding of (its) heritage'. Not least among the proposals in this report was one for the establishment and operation of a comprehensive warden service by the then proposed commission '... to be independent of sectional interests but fully integrated with them'.

For the past decade local planning authorities in Scotland have been able to include in their county development plans areas of great landscape value. These are deemed to be worthy of special protection. The pattern these areas form may be inconsistent when looked at on a national scale but, like the green belts around major towns, they are nevertheless valuable in protecting special places.

Three other bodies have been particularly significant in the development of the conservation and recreation map of Scotland. First is the Forestry Commission—beginning as long ago as 1935—with five forest parks, together covering almost 400 square miles of mainly upland country. These are Glen More, Argyll, Queen Elizabeth, Glen Trool and Kielder which extends both sides of the Border. In all of them substantial areas of unplantable and planted land

Glen More is one of five forest parks set up by the Forestry Commission in Scotland, which together cover almost 400 square miles. As a precaution against spoliation by dirt and noise, motorcars are only allowed in certain areas of the park

are available for public access, with valuable provisions for camping and other recreation activities. Here as elsewhere in Britain, the Forestry Commission has wisely prevented the motorcar from having unrestricted access to its private forest roads.

Second is the Nature Conservancy Council, already mentioned. In Scotland over the years the Council has taken into protection, among its 41 national nature reserves, a number of very large blocks of mountain land, notably the Cairngorms (64,118 acres), Inverpolly (26,837 acres) and Beinn Eighe (11,750 acres). These are either owned or held under lease or agreement with the landowners concerned, and in their character and protection are in some respects not unlike national parks. The extent to which the public have access to them varies but restrictions generally are kept to a minimum.

Third is the National Trust for Scotland, established in 1931 and now having in its care some sixty properties, including a number of important mountain areas—Torridon, Glencoe and Ben Lawers are examples. The Trust has also been active in the business of providing information about the countryside and interpreting its qualities to people, notably through a chain of well organised visitor centres running almost the length of Scotland.

To the conservation and recreation map of the 1960s two further elements have recently been added: first, country parks established under the Countryside (Scotland) Act and, second, regional parks established without the benefit of specific legislation although no less of a reality on that account.

The number of country parks is still small—four designated and developed so far. First came Culzean on the Ayrshire coast, a pleasant mixture of woodland and farmland surrounding the castle on its commanding cliff-top site. This park is managed by an unusual consortium of three local authorities and the National Trust for Scotland. There is one country park in Renfrewshire—Muirshiel; one in Dunbartonshire close to Cumbernauld New Town—Palacerigg; and one in West Lothian—Almondell and Calderwood. Others are under development, notably the Strathclyde Park, strategically located on either side of the M74 motorway in the heart of the urban conglomeration of North Lanarkshire, and planned to contain major water recreation facilities including a large rowing lake.

Regional parks, in terms of their size and character, lie somewhere between country parks (relatively small and recreation orientated) and the national park direction areas (relatively large and conservation orientated). Within them existing landscape character and traditional land uses (mainly farming) are maintained, with intensive recreational use promoted only in selected locations linked together by roads and footpaths. The most advanced of these is the Clyde-Muirshiel Regional Park in Renfrew-

shire which was started in 1967; it embraces the Muirshiel Country Park and a number of major recreation sites and has elements of a footpath system which will be extended in the future. A second regional park—in the Pentlands—has very recently been established by four local authorities, three county councils and the City Council of Edinburgh.

If 'colour on the map' is any indication of activity then at first sight Scotland's countryside might seem to be reasonably well provided for. However, much of the colour denotes a control influence—important but, in the main, negative. The national park direction areas, areas of great landscape value and green belts are all places protected to varying degrees against the wrong kind of development, but it does not follow that they are also geared to receive the ever-increasing numbers of highly mobile visitors who want to enjoy them. Until these people are adequately provided for and managed, the quality of the special places in Scotland will continue to be at risk. The problem is recognised; what is being done about it?

The Countryside (Scotland) Act, like parallel legislation in England and Wales, enables local authorities to lay on a whole range of useful facilities for informal recreation, to make access and footpath arrangements and to organise ranger services (roughly the same as the English warden services) to help visitors and to protect landowners' interests. Voluntary bodies and individual landowners too can command public funds under the same legislation, and the Countryside Commission for Scotland is able to undertake some work itself, mainly projects of a novel or experimental character which can be used as the basis for solving particular recreation problems elsewhere.

Many local authorities have taken advantage of these powers, as also have some private interests: Scotland's two regional parks are pointers to one potentially very useful element of a possible future pattern, protecting as they do landscape quality and providing for informal recreation in countryside close to major urban areas. This pattern could, with benefit, be extended to some of the relatively more remote areas of the country.

If pressures on the countryside and coast have been light enough in the past, major on-shore oil-related developments seem certain to change the pattern. In addition the creeping growth of industry and the urgent demands of tourism must somehow be satisfied without offering up rural Scotland as the hapless sacrifice.

The immediate tasks are to assess the problems right across the board, to develop a national strategy to meet the needs identified and thereafter to secure resources for implementing that strategy on a programmed basis. To this end major studies have been sponsored jointly by the Countryside Commission for Scotland, the Scottish Tourist Board and other bodies. In addition, the Commission has carried out specific studies, in consultation with other interests, for parts of three of the national park direction areas—Torridon, Glencoe and Loch Lomond—all areas where development and visitor pressures are threatening the character and beauty of the countryside. A project has been undertaken too in a fourth national park direction area—the Cairngorms—to try to develop co-operation between the field staff of existing agencies on the ground, including the Nature Conservancy Council, the Forestry Commission and private landowners, to produce a more comprehensive ranger service protection for the area.

From the knowledge obtained and still being gathered through these general and specific studies, the Commission is now developing its ideas about the feasibility of a park system for Scotland which could range from nationally select areas of fine countryside and coast where protection of existing character for public enjoyment would be the prime objective, through regional and country parks with varying intensities of recreation provision, to a linking countryside network of scenic routes, footpaths and picnic sites.

The major reorganisation of local government at present under way in Scotland, unlike the retained country organisation in England, will establish a two-tier system comprising regional and district authorities. The twelve regions will provide a more rational basis than the existing counties for considering planning needs. The regions make more logical too the establishment of regional parks, to be run by the new regional authorities, as one important element in any range of types—or system—of parks devised.

It still remains to be seen whether the future holds in store for Scotland a park system which will contain within it areas which are specifically called national parks. The dire consequences which sometimes ensue from attaching this compelling international label to special and often highly sensitive areas is readily evident elsewhere in the world. What seems significantly more important than the label is that, if these special places are designated in Scotland, they should have effective management and adequate resources to ensure their long term protection in the nation's interest. These are the immediate problems for which solutions must be found.

Much of Scotland already boasts the peace and quiet which the English and Welsh national parks are seeking to preserve through legislation. Here, near Portree on the Isle of Skye, the cliffs of Torvaig sweep down to the sea and every available piece of level ground is under cultivation

CONCLUSION

Mervyn Bell

The problems of planning and managing the national parks have proved much greater than could have been foreseen nearly a generation ago. The population of visitors to the parks, particularly those coming by car, has grown faster than the population of the country. It is now predicted that the population of Britain, which was 48.9 million in 1951 and 54.1 million in 1971, will increase to 61.2 million in 2001. The number of private cars, the main factor affecting mobility at present, has grown from 2.4 million in 1951 to 12.1 million in 1971 and on current estimates may reach 26 million in 2001. The continuing need for public transport is shown by the fact that in 1971 19.5 million, more than 1 in 3, did not have the use of a car.

Modernisation of farming and forestry practices for economic reasons, the development of electricity power stations and the supergrid transmission system, reservoirs, motorways, and greatly increased extraction of minerals have caused changes in the national parks which are hardly in accordance with the purposes for which they were established. The growing pressures upon the parks and their residents led the Government, in consultation with the Countryside Commission, to appoint the National Park Policies Review Committee in 1971 under the chairmanship of Lord Sandford, 'to review how far the national parks have fulfilled the purpose for which they were established, to consider the implications of the changes that have occurred, and may be expected, in social and economic conditions and to make recommendations as regards future policies'.

The Sandford Committee's report was published in 1974, after the preceding chapters in this book had been completed. The Committee made numerous recommendations and their report was warmly welcomed by the voluntary bodies and other park enthusiasts. At the time of writing, the report and public comment on it were being considered by the Countryside Commission and the Government. Some of the Committee's recommendations were designed to enable farmers and landowners to play a still greater part in carrying out the purposes of the national parks. Others, including 'last resort' powers of compulsory purchase, required legislation to fill gaps shown to exist in the Acts. Others again called for a change of attitude by ministers and government departments.

The scope of the Committee's recommendations was indicated by its expectation that the annual expenditure by the ten national park authorities would rise from a little over £1 million in 1971–2 to about £4 million in 1978–9. For comparison the Committee noted that in 1973–4 provision for spending on two other forms of leisure activity in England and Wales was £15 million for the Arts Council and £25 million for sport and recreation. Just how quickly national park spending rises after 1974 depends not only on implementation of the Sandford Committee's recommendations,

When the idea of national parks was first mooted in Parliament in 1929, the Cairngorms were the area which the speaker had in mind. Today, although partly under the protection of the Nature Conservancy Council, these mountains are still not designated as a national park

but also on the willingness of the new national park authorities to initiate action and contribute from the rates their 25 per cent share of the cost; their spending causes the increased amount of Exchequer grant to flow. In 1974–5 the Peak Board increased its locally borne spending by 14 per cent to take a lion's share of the Exchequer grant available. Some park authorities reduced their rate-borne expenditure, one by more than 50 per cent compared with the pre-vious year, but somewhat raised the total spent on their parks because of the greatly increased Exchequer contribution.

The Committee stressed the need for easily available funds to allow park authorities to raise money at short notice to buy property of ex-ceptional amenity or recreational value when it came onto the market. One member recom-mended a vigorous policy of land acquisition by the park authorities, and that the National Land

147

Fund, or its equivalent, should be used for purchases in national parks.

The Sandford Committee found that the sheer numbers of visitors to the parks, and the cars, coaches, caravans and powerboats they brought with them, presented the problem of people spoiling the very things they had come to enjoy. The Committee recommended that the statute dealing with the preservation and enjoyment of the parks should be amended to make it clear that the enjoyment of the national parks by the public 'shall be in such manner and by such means as will leave their natural beauty unimpaired for the enjoyment of this and future generations'. This amendment is important in that it expresses for the first time the long-cherished concept of trusteeship—the purpose of handing on unspoiled the best of what we inherit for others to enjoy.

Accepting forecasts that the overall demand for outdoor recreation was likely at least to double by the end of the century, the Committee proposed a recreation strategy which would require action within the parks by the park planning authorities, and outside them by other planning authorities. Within the parks it recommended identifying four broad categories of area in order to relate recreational use to the qualities and capacities of the land:

a areas of special importance for nature conservation, which are highly sensitive to pressure, access to which should be discouraged;

b areas of wild and relatively remote country which are of scenic and wildlife value, where access on foot, cycle or horseback is appropriate, but where penetration by motor vehicle should be limited;

c areas of good farmland and productive woodland, access to which will be limited to rights of way or other defined routes and where facilities for visitors would be self-contained, for example an enclosed picnic site;

d areas suitable for intensive recreational use which should be developed to absorb visitors, and where large scale facilities such as the major car parks and information centres should be concentrated.

The Committee added that 'recreational uses of national parks must be compatible with the qualities of the parks, among which ... a sense of tranquility and of contact with nature seems to us to be of especial value'. It recommended that, with few exceptions, provision should not be made in national parks for noisy pursuits. At the same time more picnic sites and informal country parks were needed. The question whether some of these could be linked with view points and visitor centres by scenic routes without damaging the qualities of the national parks was one which divided the Committee. But all were agreed that much more provision for the various forms of outdoor recreation that depend on a country setting was needed in all the wealth there is of fine country and coast outside the national parks. To cope with the ever-rising tide of visitors by guiding them to places where their numbers and activities would not cause damage made a regional approach essential. National park plans would need to be prepared in the context of regional and sub-regional strategies for recreation and transportation, as each affected the other.

The Committee recommended the principle that in national parks environmental quality should govern the planning of road systems, the design of alterations and the management of traffic, and explained how this should be done. Wherever possible, long-distance traffic should be routed to avoid national parks and heavy through-traffic prohibited from using roads in them. Within the parks a hierarchy of roads should be established based on their functions, and the types of vehicle to be allowed on each class of road defined. Road design and traffic management could then be sensibly related to the function and character of the roads, instead of the present system of all-purpose roads and road design based on traffic predictions.

If this principle is applied and the new definition of national park purposes understood,

The Sandford Committee Report stressed the need for more picnic sites and other recreational amenities within the national parks. Afforestation, does at least mean that such areas can be sited discreetly

decisions like the one made in 1973 to enlarge the Lake District National Park section of the A66 to motorway size will surely not be possible. Happily an example of putting the principle into practice also comes from the Lake District. The county surveyor and the county planning officer jointly recommended a design speed of 45mph and a maximum road width of 24ft for the seven-mile stretch of the A591 between Windermere and Grasmere, so

that road improvements would be restrained to keep the road in scale with the scenery through which it passes.

The Committee recommended that road improvements should require planning consent. If this were accepted, the character of roads including minor roads would be maintained, and traffic management, which has the great advantage of flexibility, would become the principal remedy for congestion. At peak

149

periods greater use of minibuses to carry visitors from their parked cars to beauty spots like the Goyt Valley, was envisaged by the Committee. People who did not have cars, or who wanted to leave them and walk, should, it said, be helped by more bus services in holiday periods. Examples were the experimental services sponsored by the park authorities and the Countryside Commission in the Northumberland, Peak District and Pembrokeshire Coast National Parks, and the independent Mountain Goat service in the Lake District which caters for residents all the year round.

Powers to grant or refuse planning consent under the Town and Country Planning Acts have been the main means available to the park planning authorities for protecting the natural beauty of the parks. The Sandford Committee considered that the park authorities had on the whole successfully preserved local character in dealing with the great bulk of residential and small scale commercial development, but needed to insist on higher standards of design. The authorities should, it said, have a fresh look at their development control policies and apply them more strictly in the face of the growing pressures for residential and tourist development; unsightly caravan camps should be relocated. Expressing some surprise that it had not already been done, the Committee recommended that the Landscape Areas Special Development Order of 1950, which enabled park authorities to consider the design and materials of new farm buildings in much of Snowdonia and the Lake District and part of the Peak District, should be extended to the whole of every national park and that it should also cover siting.

The main burden of complaint to the Committee was directed against the many major developments there had been in the parks, such as the Fylingdales Early Warning Station and the Boulby potash mine in the North York Moors, the power station at Trawsfynydd in Snowdonia, the television mast at Hessary Tor in Dartmoor, and in exploiting natural resources of water and minerals. They had been permitted 'in the national interest', after full inquiry and public discussion, and the decisions had usually been made by ministers, occasionally by Parliament. The Committee believed that although such developments were sometimes unavoidable, '... amenity values are intangible and may on that account all too easily be outweighed in the minds of those taking decisions by the more readily quantified benefits expected from various forms of incongruous development'. It emphasised that large scale industrial development was in fundamental conflict with the purposes of national parks, however skilfully it might be carried out.

Because the national parks amount to 9 per cent of the entire area of England and Wales, contain valuable minerals and form a large part of the best water-gathering grounds, the Committee concluded that it would be unrealistic to declare national parks 'inviolate'. It said:

> The presumption against development which would be out of accord with park purposes must be strong throughout the whole of the parks; in the most beautiful parts which remain unspoiled it should amount to a prohibition to be breached only in the case of a compelling national necessity.

If large scale industrial development is in fundamental conflict with the purposes of national parks, what about military training in them? Large parts of three of the national parks (Northumberland, 22 per cent; Dartmoor, 5 per cent; Pembrokeshire Coast, 5 per cent) are owned or leased by the Ministry of Defence and used by the armed services for all forms of training. Some of these akin to 'adventure training' may be in harmony with national park purposes, but certainly not live firing, the use of tracked vehicles and low flying. In some of the other parks there are smaller holdings.

The Sandford Committee did not investigate the problems, because another committee, the Defence Lands Review Committee, with Lord Nugent as chairman, had been appointed by the Government. Its report was published in 1973 and at the time of writing was still being considered by the Government.

The Nugent Report hardly lived up to the theme of the Prime Minister's speech, 'Choices and Opportunities', when he announced his intention to appoint a review committee to the final 'Countryside in 1970' conference. The Committee limited its choices by trying to do its job of reducing 'the demands of the Services on land, particularly in places like national parks ...' wholly within the existing Defence estate. It recommended release of only 3,269 acres out of a holding of 76,700 acres in national parks (2 per cent of their total area).

Some members of the Sandford Committee recommended that no new defence holding or intensification of existing service use should be permitted in or adjoining national parks without a public inquiry, and that holdings in the parks should be stringently reviewed every five years. One member recommended that the objective of the reviews should be to secure the progressive removal of the Ministry of Defence from the parks, and its land handed over to the national park authorities.

The use of land for agriculture and forestry, the two wholly rural occupations which support the life of the residents of the parks, is not 'development' and therefore exempt from planning control. Consultation procedures, largely informal, have been encouraged as a substitute. Forestry has become a major land-use in the national parks since 1945. The Forestry Commission is now the largest single landowner holding 205,100 acres (6 per cent of the total area of the parks), a few thousand acres more than the National Trust controls. The planting of conifers by the Forestry Commission and private interests on bare land in the uplands and the replacing of uneconomic broad leaved woods in the valleys have made great changes in the characteristic appearance of the parks.

The Sandford Committee found deep concern among farming, amenity and recreation groups at the prospect of continued afforestation of bare land and considered that the arrangements for consultation of the park authorities by the Forestry Commission and private interests had proved an inadequate safeguard of national park interests. It believed that afforestation could be acceptable, provided that it was not prominent in the landscape and was properly integrated with farming use; but the familiar appearance and recreational use of parts of the parks, in some cases very substantial parts, had been adversely affected. The Committee recommended that the afforestation of bare land in national parks should be made subject to planning control, and it expected that national park authorities would increasingly accept responsibility for broad leaved woods.

Overall forestry policy was being separately reviewed by the Government while the Sandford Committee was sitting and consideration of the Committee's recommendations on forestry in national parks was apparently overtaken by a government announcement made three months after its report was published. The Minister of Agriculture, announcing a new dedication scheme designed to encourage hardwood planting by private timber growers, explained that arrangements for consultation of amenity, conservation, planning and farming interests would be strengthened with a view to securing agreement on all forestry proposals.

The great importance of farming to the purposes of national parks was stressed by the Sandford Committee:

Grazing maintains the characteristic open landscapes, which delight the eye and favour the foot. Arable or mown fields in the valleys with well maintained walls and buildings enrich the scene. The discerning visitor also relishes glimpses of a life very different from his own and, if he is fortunate, contact with some of the personalities it produces.

The parks depend especially upon prosperous hill farming and the Committee found the prospects reasonably good. The Ministry of Agriculture advised that entry into the European Economic Community would stimulate home production of meat, so there would be more sheep and cattle in the hills. But, the Committee believed, some changes would be in conflict with park purposes, particularly the conversion of rough, open country to enclosed, cultivated land. The improvement of rough grazing to better grazing, pasture or arable, had already significantly affected public enjoyment of the scenery and of opportunities to walk freely in open country in Exmoor, the North York Moors and Dartmoor. In the other parks, which had been much less affected, it concluded that the main change to be expected would be the introduction of controlled grazing, which required fencing, but that it would not be on any large scale in their open country.

The Committee recommended that much more attention should be given to co-ordinating agricultural and environmental policies, both in the European Economic Community and at home. It expected that most of the conflicts between farming and national park purposes would be resolved by agreement; the objective should be to ensure that the land would continue in farming use, but in a manner acceptable to the park authority.

The Committee proposed a new form of management agreement to supplement the use of access agreements in open country, with payments to the owners for purposes such as the active maintenance of a particular kind of ground cover such as heather, or continued grazing where it had become unprofitable. Such management agreements (the 'landscape agreements' which were originally proposed by the Countryside Commission) would have wide application, not limited to open country. The Committee considered that an owner who did not wish to do what was asked of him should be able to compel the park authority to buy his land. It further recommended, since he could legally insist on doing what he liked with his land by way of agriculture or forestry, that the national park authority should have a new last-resort power to purchase compulsorily open country in order to conserve its natural beauty, subject to the usual rights of objection and to confirmation by the Secretary of State. A majority of the members recommended that the power should extend to any land in a national park; without it the park authorities could not, in the last resort, give effect to the first purpose for which the parks had been established.

The Committee considered that a much more positive attitude by national park authorities towards the making of access agreements was overdue, and that except for the Lake District and the Peak District they needed to develop much stronger and wider ranging warden services. These two parks had exceptionally large numbers of visitors, but complaints about public behaviour were few.

After a slow start, because the Commission had no funds to support them until 1961–2, forty information centres had been established in the parks by the end of 1972, but the North York Moors and Dartmoor still had no centres in permanent buildings. Because of the great benefit information and interpretative services brought both for the public and for the conservation of the parks, the Committee recommended that a major effort should be made to improve and extend them. It emphasised, too, the need for a continuing interchange of information and experience between the park authority and local people, who were often the first to notice the effects of visitor needs for which provision had not been made. The Committee recommended the creation of advisory panels for each park, or perhaps a single larger body, to provide a recognised means for consultation and two-way exchange of ideas between the park authority and the bodies representing local landowning, farming and timber-growing interests, parish and community councils, and voluntary amenity and conservation societies.

The Sandford Committee's great concern about the growing pressures and demands upon the parks, and the degrading that had already happened to parts of them, led four members to propose a new procedure for identifying and giving special protection to 'national heritage areas' in parts of national parks which have 'exceptionally high environmental qualities un-

The problem of afforestation looms large in all the national parks. Here, at Capel Curig in Snowdonia, the conifer plantation seems inoffensive, elsewhere, as for example on Exmoor, such a development could completely ruin the character of the park

impaired by intrusive development or incongruous uses'. Relatively small, there might be several of them in each national park, the best of mountain and moor, sea cliffs and islands and so on. Amenity would always prevail in them; there would be no quarrying, mining, reservoirs, defence works, main roads or railways, and no facilities for visitors except carefully sited map boards and emergency shelters. Management agreements would be negotiated gradually with owners, including the National Trust and public bodies such as the Nature Conservancy Council, to protect the environmental qualities in perpetuity. Designation by the Countryside Commission when confirmed by Government would thereafter prohibit development or incongruous change of use unless permitted by Parliament. The cost would be borne by the Exchequer.

Four other members considered the proposal unsound and unnecessary. They argued that each park should be administered as a unity; that yet another and superior category of protected area would unavoidably depreciate the status of all the remaining park in the minds of both public and decision takers; and that the accolade of special designation would bring the public pouring into it. They were satisfied that the conservation of the qualities of the most beautiful and unspoiled parts of the parks could be secured by the new national park authorities, using the existing procedures and the new powers proposed by the Committee. They believed that resources of money and management were needed even more in the country surrounding the heritage areas; the settings rather than the gems were at risk.

The differences there were between the members of the Committee were about means not ends. All were convinced that the wish of a great and growing volume of public opinion to preserve and enhance the qualities of the national parks for present and future generations could be achieved, 'but only if in future our national parks and their purposes are taken much more seriously by all concerned, not least by local authorities and government departments'.

What distinguishes the national parks from other areas of great beauty is that in the parks fine scenery and wild remoter country are combined. This is their special contribution. And there is growing understanding of the need for such places of retreat from the stresses of modern living; the need for sanctuaries for men and women as well as wildlife in a crowded island. It is a need that we cannot ignore.

BIBLIOGRAPHY

DARTMOOR

Burrows, R. *The Naturalist in Devon and Cornwall* (Newton Abbot, 1971)

Crossing, William. *Guide to Dartmoor* (1912, reprinted Newton Abbot, 1965)

Devon County Council. *Dartmoor National Park Policy Plan* (1973)

Hoskins, W. G. (ed). *Dartmoor National Park Guide* (HMSO, 1957)

Perkins, J. W. *Geology Explained: Dartmoor and the Tamar Valley* (Newton Abbot, 1972)

Sayer, S. *Wild Country: National Asset or Barren Waste?* (Exeter, 1972)

A descriptive list of all known books on Dartmoor subjects is provided by *The Dartmoor Bibliography* compiled by J. V. Somers Cocks, Dartmoor Preservation Association, 1971.

EXMOOR

Burton, S. H. *Exmoor* (1969, new edition, 1974)

Coleman-Cooke, John (ed). *Exmoor National Park Guide* (HMSO, 1970)

Lloyd, E. R. *The Wild Red Deer of Exmoor* (Dulverton, 1970)

MacDermot, E. T. *The History of the Forest of Exmoor* (Newton Abbot, 1973)

Page, J. Ll. W. *An Exploration of Exmoor* (1890)

Sinclair, G. *The Vegetation of Exmoor* (Dulverton, 1970)

Whybrow, C. *Antiquary's Exmoor* (Dulverton, 1970)

BRECON BEACONS

Brecknock County Naturalists' Trust. *Breconshire Naturalist*, published as their *Bulletin* from 1964

Davies, Margaret (ed). *Brecon Beacons National Park Guide* (HMSO, 1972)

Hadfield, Charles. *The Canals of South Wales and the Border* (Cardiff, 1960)

Hurley, L. F. *The National Park in Monmouthshire* (Brecon, 1963)

Hyde, A. H. and Guile, D. P. M. *Plant Life in Brecknock* (Brecknock Museum, 1962)

North, F. J. 'The Brecon Beacons', *Britain's National Parks* (1959)

Savory, H. N. 'The Prehistory of Brecknock', *Brycheiniog*, 1 (1955)

PEMBROKESHIRE COAST

Barrett, John H. 'The Birds of the Parish of Dale', *Field Studies*, 1 (1959)

———. *The Pembrokeshire Coast Long Distance Path* (HMSO, 1974)

Davies, T. A. Warren. *The Plants of Pembrokeshire* (Haverfordwest, 1970)

George, Barbara. 'Pembrokeshire Sea-trading before 1900', *Field Studies*, 2 (1964)

Miles, Dillwyn (ed). *Pembrokeshire Coast National Park Guide* (HMSO, 1973)

SNOWDONIA

Edwards, G. Rhys. *Snowdonia National Park*, Snowdonia National Park Joint Advisory Committee (1970)

Forrest, H. E. *The Vertebrate Fauna of North Wales* (1907, 1919)

Vale, Edmund (ed). *Snowdonia National Park Guide* (HMSO, 1968)

Watson, Katherine. *North Wales*, Regional Archaeologies series (1967)

Williams, H. 'The Geology of Snowdon', *Quart Journ Geol Soc*, *83* (1927)

PEAK DISTRICT

Boyd, D. F. and Monkhouse, P. J. *Walking in the Pennines* (Glasgow, 1937)

Clapham, A. R. (ed). *Flora of Derbyshire* (1969)

Ford, T. D. and others (eds). *The Caves of Derbyshire* (revised edition, Clapham, 1967)

155

BIBLIOGRAPHY

Hams, H. *Industrial Archaeology of the Peak District* (Newton Abbot, 1971)

Monkhouse, Patrick (ed). *Peak District National Park Guide* (HMSO, 1960)

Stephenson, Tom. *The Pennine Way* (HMSO, 1969)

Tarn, Prof J. N. *The Peak National Park—Its Architecture*, Peak Park Planning Board (1971)

LAKE DISTRICT

Fell, Clare. *Early Settlement in the Lake Counties* (Clapham, 1972)

Hervey, G. A. K. and Barnes, J. A. G. (eds). *Natural History of the Lake District* (1970)

Millward, Roy and Robinson, Adrian. *Cumbria*, Landscapes of Britain series (1972)

Pearsall, W. H. (ed). *The Lake District National Park Guide* (HMSO, 1969)

—— and Pennington, W. *The Lake District*, New Naturalist series (1973)

Rollinson, William. *A History of Man in the Lake District* (1967)

Wordsworth, William. *A Guide through the District of the Lakes* (5th edition, 1835, reprinted Oxford, 1970)

YORKSHIRE DALES

Chislett, R. *Yorkshire Birds* (1952)

Hartley, M. and Ingilby, J. *Life and Tradition in the Yorkshire Dales* (1968)

Longworth, I. H. *Yorkshire*, Regional Archaeologies series (1965)

Raistrick, A. *Old Yorkshire Dales* (1968)

Ramblers' Association. *Rambles in the Dales* (Nelson, 1968)

Simmons, I. G. (ed). *Yorkshire Dales National Park Guide* (HMSO, 1971)

Speakman, C. *The Dales Way* (Clapham, 1970)

NORTH YORK MOORS

Blakeborough, R. *Wit, Character, Folklore and Customs of the North Riding* (1898, reprinted Wakefield, 1973)

Bonser, K. J. *The Drovers* (1970)

Falconer, A. *The Cleveland Way* (HMSO, 1972)

——. *Motoring on the North York Moors* (Clapham, 1973)

Marr, Anthony. *Climber's Guide to the North York Moors* (Goring, 1970)

Mee, A. *Yorkshire, North Riding*, King's England series (1941)

Ramblers' Association. *Walking on the North York Moors* (Clapham, 1973)

Raistrick, A. (ed). *North York Moors National Park Guide* (HMSO, 1966)

NORTHUMBERLAND

Birley, A. R. *Hadrian's Wall: An Illustrated Guide* (HMSO, 1963)

Bolam, G. *The Birds of Northumberland and the Eastern Borders* (Alnwick, 1912)

Clark, W. A. 'Afforestation and Conservation in Northumberland', in *The Conservation of the British Flora*, Bot Soc Brit Isles (1963)

Mee, A. *Northumberland*, King's England series (1952)

Phillipson, J. (ed). *Northumberland National Park Guide* (HMSO, 1969)

Robinson, D. A. *A Guide to the Geology of Northumberland and the Borders*, Nat Hist Soc Northumberland and Durham (1965)

ACKNOWLEDGEMENTS

The plates in this volume are reproduced by kind permission of the following:

Barnaby's Picture Library: pp 20, 52, 62, 64, 71, 75, 76, 87, 99, 109, 145, 153 and 155

British Tourist Authority: pp 13 and 149

J. Allan Cash: pp 27, 40, 47, 50, 131 and 137

Evening Gazette: pp 121, 123 and 124

Leonard and Marjorie Gayton: pp 36 and 39

Geographical Magazine: pp 24, 60, 83, 88, 101, 111 and 113

Popperfoto: p 95

Radio Times Hulton Picture Library: pp 6, 9 and 16

John Topham Picture Library: pp 134, 142 and 147

The maps were drawn by Susan Rowland for the *Geographical Magazine*

INDEX

Places of interest are followed by the name of the park where they are situated. The following abbreviations should be noted:

NYM	North York Moors	Sn	Snowdonia	Lakes	Lake District
PD	Peak District	BB	Brecon Beacons	Nd	Northumberland
Pembs	Pembrokeshire Coast	Dart	Dartmoor	Y	Yorkshire Dales
Scot	Scotland	Ex	Exmoor		

Page references in italics refer to illustrations

Abereiddi (Pembs), *62*

Access to Mountains (Scotland) Bill, 6, 140

Agen Allwedd Caves (BB), 54

Angle Peninsula (Pembs), 65

Arbor Low (PD), 85

Areas of outstanding natural beauty, 9

Arennig Peaks (Sn), 69

Argyll Park (Scot), 141

Armondell and Calderwood Country Park (Scot), 143

Beaker folk, 35, 49, 74, 133

Beinn Eighe Nature Reserve (Scot), 142

Ben Lawers (Scot), 143

Betws-y-coed (Sn), 73

Birkdale Pass (Y), 107

Black Mountain (BB), 43

Bodmin Moor (Dart), 17

Brecknock, forest of (BB), 43-4

Brecon (BB), *47*

Brecon Beacons, 10, 42-55: biological interests, 48; Bronze and Iron Ages, 49; cave systems, 54; depopulation, 51; Devonian scarps, 44-6; easy access, 52-3; Fforest Fawr, 51; geology, 43-6; lakes, 47; main features, 42; map, 44-5; nature reserves, 48; neolithics, 48-9; Norman invasion, 49-50; reservoirs, 51; river system, 47-8

Broads, Norfolk, 10

Buxton Railway (PD), *83*, 88

Bwlch Tyddiad Pass (Sn), 75

Byland Abbey (NYM), 119

Cadair Idris (Sn), 69

Cairngorms (Scot), 141, 142, *147*

Cambrian Mountains National Park, 10

Cantref Reservoir (BB), 48

Capel Curig (Sn), *153*

Carneddau Hengwm graves (Sn), 73

Chapman Barrows (Ex), 35

Chee Tor (PD), 82

Cheviot Hills (Nd), 10, 128, 130, 132

Cleddau Estuary (Pembs), 63

Cleveland Hills (NYM), 117, 120

Combestone Tor (Dart), *20*

Commons, Open Spaces and Footpaths Preservation Society, 6, 97

Conclusion of the study, 146-55

Conservation Areas, 9-10

Coquet (Nd), 128, 132

Cornish Coast, 10

Cornwall, Duchy of, 23-4

Council for the Preservation of Rural England, 7

Countryside Commission (1968), 8, 11

Countryside (Scotland) Act, 1967, 141, 143

Craig Cerrig Gleisiad (BB), 43

Craig y Dinas (Sn), 74

Crib Goch (Sn), 67, *71*

Culzean Country Park (Scot), 143

Cwm Eigiau Valley (Sn), 69

Cwm Idwal (Sn), 67, 69

Cymer Abbey (Sn), 76

Dales, The (PD), 82

Dartmeet (Dart), *27*

Dartmoor, 10, 11, 15, 17-29: abbeys, 22; Bronze Age, 22; climate, 21; farmers, 21, 25; farm-houses, 25-6; kists, 22; *main features*, 17; map, 18; medieval iron-smelting, 22; minerals, 19-20, 25; mining, 23-4; ponies, 21, 24; railway system, 28 ·

Devil's Elbow (Scot), 140

Devil's Frying-pan (Dart), 21

Devil's Kitchen (Sn), 67

Devonian scarps (BB), 45

Dodd Fell (Y), 105

Doone Valley (Ex), *40*

Dovedale (PD), 82, 84

Dove river (NYM), 117

Dower, John, 8-9, 14-15, 128

Dunkery Beacon (Ex), 34, *36*

Easby Moor (NYM), 117

Elishaw (Nd), 133

Elsdon Castle (Nd), 135

Eskdale (Lakes), 92

Exmoor, 10, 11, 15, 30-41: area included, 31; Bronze and Iron Ages, 35; farming, 31, 38; forest of, 36-7; geography, 34-5; *main features*, 30; map, 31-3; people of, 31, 34; recreations, 40; red deer, 34; topography, 41

Farndale, proposed reservoir at (NYM), 120, 125-6

Farm lands within national parks, 15-16

Fat Betty Cross (NYM), 119

Fell Sandstones (Nd), 130, 133

Foel Trigarn Fort (Pembs), 60

Fylingdale Moor (NYM), *124*

Garn Fawr Fort (Pembs), 60

Glen More Park (Scot), 141, 142

Glen Trool Park (Scot), 141-2

Goyt Valley (PD), *88*, 89

Grange-over-Sands (Lakes), 100

Grasmere (Lakes), 95

Greta Valley (Y), 105

Hadrian's Wall (Nd), 128, 133, *134*

Haddon Hall (PD), 84

Hambleton Horse, Kilburn (NYM), 122